WEST ACADEMIC
EMERITUS

JESSE H. CHOPER
Professor of Law and Dean Emeritus
University of California, Berkeley

LARRY D. KRAMER
President, William and Flora Hewlett Foundation

GRANT S. NELSON
Professor of Law Emeritus, Pepperdine University
Professor of Law Emeritus, University of California, Los Angeles

JAMES J. WHITE
Robert A. Sullivan Emeritus Professor of Law
University of Michigan

West Academic Publishing's Law School Advisory Board

MARK C. ALEXANDER
Arthur J. Kania Dean and Professor of Law
Villanova University Charles Widger School of Law

JOSHUA DRESSLER
Distinguished University Professor Emeritus
Michael E. Moritz College of Law, The Ohio State University

MEREDITH J. DUNCAN
Professor of Law
University of Houston Law Center

RENÉE McDONALD HUTCHINS
Dean & Professor of Law
University of Maryland Carey School of Law

RENEE KNAKE JEFFERSON
Joanne and Larry Doherty Chair in Legal Ethics &
Professor of Law, University of Houston Law Center

ORIN S. KERR
William G. Simon Professor of Law
University of California, Berkeley

JONATHAN R. MACEY
Professor of Law,
Yale Law School

DEBORAH JONES MERRITT
Distinguished University Professor,
John Deaver Drinko/Baker & Hostetler Chair in Law Emerita
Michael E. Moritz College of Law, The Ohio State University

ARTHUR R. MILLER
University Professor and Chief Justice Warren E. Burger Professor of
Constitutional Law and the Courts, New York University

A. BENJAMIN SPENCER
Dean & Trustee Professor of Law
William & Mary Law School

1L SUCCESS: BECOMING A LAWYER

A Professional Identity Formation Workbook

Sara J. Berman

Professor of Lawyering Skills and Director of Academic Success
University of Southern California, Gould School of Law

WEST ACADEMIC

The publisher is not engaged in rendering legal or other professional advice, and this publication is not a substitute for the advice of an attorney. If you require legal or other expert advice, you should seek the services of a competent attorney or other professional.

© 2024 LEG, Inc. d/b/a West Academic
    860 Blue Gentian Road, Suite 350
    Eagan, MN 55121
    1-877-888-1330

West, West Academic Publishing, and West Academic are trademarks of West Publishing Corporation, used under license.

Published in the United States of America

ISBN: 978-1-68561-331-0

This book is dedicated to Ira & Evelyne who gave me the love, space, and support to write this book.

ACKNOWLEDGMENTS

To Neil Hamilton, Jerry Organ, and everyone connected with the Holloran Center and to all supporters of the Professional Identity Formation movement in legal education. I know I speak for many when I share how fulfilling it was to find thoughts I'd had since law school put into books, articles, convenings, and, most recently ABA Standards. I recall as if it were yesterday, more than a decade ago when my now dear friend David Thomson was answering the question at an AALS panel: what are the differences between professionalism, professional responsibility, and professional identity? Detailed answers to that question along with databases cataloguing the growing body of related research can be found at the Holloran Center at https://law.stthomas.edu/about/centers-institutes/holloran-center/ and https://law.stthomas.edu/about/centers-institutes/holloran-center/research-training/professional-formation/index.html.

As professionals we are lifelong learners, so I acknowledge with infinite gratitude my many "teachers"—including former professors, friends, family, and too many colleagues to name.

I must acknowledge with profound and particular appreciation Professor Jerry Organ (noted above) for reading and discussing the manuscript and Professor Lauren Hespos from Touro Law Center for her eagle-eyed review.

Lastly, I extend my profound and heartfelt thanks to my visionary publisher Pamela Siege Chandler and to my brilliant editors, John Moen, Megan Putler, Louis Higgins and the entire editorial team at West, including special thanks to the production team with Laura Holle, Whitney Esson, Michele Bassett, Megan Hoffman, and Rebecca Schneider.

And to law students everywhere; you are fiduciaries for our future.

FOREWORD

By Professor Jerry Organ—January 2024, Minneapolis, MN

Sara Berman has years of experience working with thousands of law students to help them find success in law school. This book represents the accumulated wisdom that Berman is sharing to support the next generation of law students on their journey from law student to lawyer.

This book is a recipe for "success" on multiple levels. In chapter after chapter, Berman shares a multitude of insights on how to find "success" as a law student—on how to be a more effective law student—including reading techniques, study habits both before and after exams, and a constant emphasis on having a growth mindset and a positive attitude.

Even moreso, however, Berman provides countless opportunities for students to learn more about themselves—to understand their "why"—and to reflect on the steps they are taking on their journey from law student to lawyer so that they can enjoy the "success" of being the lawyer they hope and want to be. Berman also encourages law students to be cognizant of the importance of self-care—so that they can develop good well-being habits as they progress from law student to lawyer.

By emphasizing practical academic skills and encouraging self-understanding and meta-cognition, Berman gives law students the tools to achieve greater academic success while also providing them the framework and encouragement to find the success associated with discovering the distinct and fulfilling way they are meant to serve clients as a lawyer.

Jerome M. Organ
Bakken Professor of Law and Co-Director of the
Holloran Center for Ethical Leadership in the Professions
University of St. Thomas School of Law
1000 LaSalle Ave., MSL303
Minneapolis, MN 55403
jmorgan@stthomas.edu

INTRODUCTION

Congratulations! Your life is about to change. You are not just "going" to law school. You have embarked on a legal education journey of lifelong learning. Your identity is already in transformation. You are *becoming* a lawyer. You are working to *earn* a degree and professional license that will *open* future doors and create a lifetime of opportunity.

Your education is powerful and precious; no one can ever take it away. When you fully invest in this new law school world—meaning when you get to know the people, take chances, and use the incredible resources available to you—not only will you learn rules of law, legal reasoning, and lawyering skills, you will become part of something bigger.

You will never see yourself or the world around you the same. You will learn a different language and think about things in a different manner. People will seek your advice. And, you will have critically important choices to make about who you want to be as a lawyer and leader.

First-Year Law Students (1Ls): This Is for You

This workbook is *written for you and to you*. It is not a rule book or skills guide. There are plenty of those. I will recommend some great ones, and faculty and librarians in your law school will recommend others.

This is also not a scholarly work on professional identity formation; you can find many of those referenced in sources in the Acknowledgements above.

You might think of this book as a conversation with a law school success coach. We'll focus together on clearing the way for you to do *your* very best, and enjoy the process, as you embark on and proceed along your legal education journey.

You can read and work through parts of this workbook before law school to get a head start, during your first semester as you delve into classes and prepare for your first set of law school exams, and in your second semester to improve upon first semester grades, re-focus habits, better manage time and stress, and more successfully cope with other law school challenges. I hope the book also helps you find greater fulfillment along the way.

This workbook will also help families, friends, spouses, and partners of law students to see why law school is so different and so difficult, and to understand how best to learn to lend a hand, or back off, as needed. *Friends and family: as key players in the life of a law student, your support is critical. So, thank you!*

Let's start here. Going to law school is like spending three years abroad—the language, customs, rules, and, well, basically everything is different. Law schools, like foreign countries, have their own:

- Governments, with administrations headed by deans, faculty committees, boards of directors or advisory boards, student organizations, and alumni groups;
- Laws, including a student handbook, faculty handbook, honor code, internal policies, and external standards from accrediting bodies such as the ABA and state and regional accreditors;
- Leadership including administrators, faculty, professional staff, student leaders;
- History, with institutional history (some unwritten and some noted in meeting minutes and law school magazines) and alumni/professor stories about how things used to be;
- Customs inside the law school and in the greater legal education and professional communities; and
- Language with terminology, jargon, slang, acronyms, and abbreviations.

Feeling that you *belong* in this new world does *not* happen just because you get in the door. You can travel to a foreign country and stay in an American hotel, eat American foods, and never even talk with locals! Or, you can live abroad, work to really get to know the people, and become part of a new

INTRODUCTION xi

community and culture. When you immerse yourself, you become richer; a part of that new country stays with you forever.

Similarly, when you invest yourself fully in law school, far above and beyond the already significant monetary investment you are making, you become part of the legal profession for life, and it becomes a part of you. My hope is that will all be for the better.

It is OK, though, if at first law school feels overwhelming. No, it's more than OK; **it is totally normal!** Even if you succeeded in every previous academic endeavor (maybe especially if you did), it's perfectly reasonable to wonder *and worry* here. But almost everyone who starts law school finishes and graduates. Likely, you will too. It won't be easy, but it will be immensely rewarding.

Professional Identity Formation

There are many excellent books about law school. Some focus on rules of law, others on skills. This workbook is a success companion guide; it provides strategies to excel in the law school environment and dedicatd space to process your own personal reflections and contextualize the transformation you are undergoing as you work toward becoming a lawyer. Law school has not traditionally provided space for such reflection, but I believe it is important; hence, this workbook.

We will be realistic, but we will focus on making your legal education journey a positive and empowering experience.

ABA standards were recently updated to include that, "a law school shall provide substantial opportunities to students for . . . the development of a professional identity." According to the ABA's interpretation of Standard 303(b):

> "[P]rofessional identity focuses on what it means to be a lawyer and the special obligations lawyers have to their clients and society. The development of a professional identity should involve an intentional exploration of the values, guiding principles, and well-being practices considered foundational to successful legal practice. Because developing a professional identity requires reflection and growth over time,

students should have frequent opportunities during each year of law school and in a variety of courses and co-curricular and professional development activities."

At the same time, the ABA also added a provision to Standard 303 that, "[a] law school shall provide education to law students on bias, cross-cultural competency, and racism: (1) at the start of the program of legal education, and (2) at least once again before graduation." (Standard 303(c).) The ABA states:

> "[T]he importance of cross-cultural competence to professionally responsible representation and the obligation of lawyers to promote a justice system that provides equal access and eliminates bias, discrimination, and racism in the law should be among the values and responsibilities of the legal profession to which students are introduced."

Throughout this workbook, you'll find opportunities for self-reflection about your professional identity formation ("PIF") and cross-cultural competency ("CCC"), including learning to improve your ability to effectively communicate and work as a future lawyer with people whose backgrounds differ from yours.

You may work through these PIF and/or CCC reflections independently or as part of class or workshop. You can keep your completed reflections in a dedicated PIF folder on your laptop, or complete these in notes on your phone just for you. And, you can return to these later in law school and in practice to get back in touch with your earlier thinking. You will be amazed at your own transformation—and/or at how your core values may well remain the same.

Why focus on PIF? Not just because the ABA says law schools must incorporate this training, but because seeing your legal education journey through professional lenses will help you:

- Focus on the bigger picture beyond day-to-day challenges,
- Remain positive,
- Find deeper meaning that will keep you inspired and moving forward, and

INTRODUCTION   xiii

- Become the lawyer you want to be, someone whose actions are aligned not only with formal rules of professional responsibility but with your own values and beliefs.

In short, this perspective will help you succeed now and serve clients well when you graduate, cultivating habits and perspectives that will lead to a lifetime of professional satisfaction.

What you *do* and how you *think*, your actions *and* your mindset as you proceed on this journey, will help get you through today's struggles and will pay success dividends for decades to come. Especially when something is tough, and it will be, or when you feel you don't belong, or when a concept is so confusing that you get a headache trying to understand it, you will stay more balanced, motivated, and hopefully happy(!) when you use the tools we will discuss throughout this book.

Two examples of many strategies we will return to are:

- Reframing "problems" as "opportunities," sometimes even "gifts," and,
- Pausing or "taking a beat" (or taking time to breathe) in the heat of particularly stressful moments. Sometimes even just the tiniest "pause" will provide the distance to see that many daily "battles" just won't be that significant in the long run. (*Will this matter five days or five years from now?*)

Much of what we will talk about and reflect on in this workbook is personal and unique to you. This is *your* success journey. You are very much on your own path. I'm not going to tell you what to do or how to think; I am going to suggest strategies for you to use as you see fit, to enhance your awareness, focus your priorities, and thrive in the face of the inevitable challenges. And I'll celebrate with you as you make mistakes, overcome them, and settle into professional success (whatever that means to you).

Now, I know you may just be starting 1L, but let's play a backward design game for a moment. After graduation, when you are licensed, what will it mean for you to be a lawyer?

A couple of caveats before the reflection:

1) The book refers to becoming a lawyer. There are many wonderful ways to earn a living with a law degree other than practicing law. We find lawyers in every slice of life including business and education, politics and government, sports and the arts, communications, and hospitality. But because our identity is so profound, many of us continue to think of ourselves as lawyers, perhaps "non-practicing lawyers," even as we work in other professional capacities. So, for readers who are not sure you want to work as a lawyer after graduation, all good! Keep reading and completing the reflections throughout this book. And, any time you want to substitute the word, "lawyer" with whatever best describes your professional vision, go right ahead.

2) Throughout the book, we refer to walking, movement, and other physical exercise. Please know that implied in those references is "if or as you are able and comfortable with." Nowhere do I mean to exclude or be disrespectful.

3) On a similar note, language is constantly changing. I have tried throughout this workbook to write in an inclusive and respectful manner. But, cross cultural competency is a lifelong learning process for us all, myself included. So, if you have suggestions for future editions, please drop me a line.

Alright, time for action. Take out your phone, laptop, or a pen and paper and complete this first PIF Reflection. Don't think, just write. This is for your eyes only. We'll revisit these questions later in the book, and your responses may well change. No problem! Just take out your phone or a pen and put down the first words that come to mind.

INTRODUCTION

PIF Reflection: Find Your "Why"

What does "becoming a lawyer" mean for you?

What changes have you noticed in yourself since you started law school?

What do you see changing throughout your law school years? (You may not be able to answer this question yet, but give it a try; your thoughts, concerns, and insights might surprise you.)

What do you see changing in your life once you have a law license?

ABOUT THE AUTHOR

Sara J. Berman is a professor of lawyering skills at the USC Gould School of Law. Berman's areas of scholarship include student success and high stakes test preparation.

Berman's publications include:

- Bar Exam Success: A Comprehensive Guide, 2d ed. (West Academic)
- First-Year Law Students Exam Success: A Comprehensive Guide (West Academic)
- Bar Exam MPT Preparation & Experiential Learning For Law Students: Interactive Performance Test Training, 2d (West Academic)
- Step-by-Step Guide to Criminal Law, co-authored with Steve Bracci (West Academic)
- Step-by-Step Guide to Torts, co-authored with Steve Bracci (West Academic)
- Step-by-Step Guide to Contracts, co-authored with Steve Bracci (West Academic)
- Represent Yourself in Court: How to Prepare and Try a Winning Case, 12th ed., co-authored with Paul Bergman (published by Nolo.com)
- The Criminal Law Handbook: Know Your Rights, Survive the System, 18th ed., co-authored with Paul Bergman (published by Nolo.com)
- Office Hours on Academic Success (West Academic)

Table of Contents

Acknowledgments V

Foreword VII

Introduction IX

About the Author XVII

Chapter 1. Before Law School—and Orientation 1

Chapter 2. Start on a Positive Foot: Your Path Is Not Pre-Destined 9

Chapter 3. Become a Critical Reader 17

Chapter 4. Find Your Why 25

Chapter 5. Hard Work Is the Most Important Part of Success 29

Chapter 6. Visualize Yourself as a Lawyer 35

Chapter 7. Enhance Focus, Reduce Distractions 39

Chapter 8. Active Learning 53

Chapter 9. Surround Yourself with Positive People 59

Chapter 10. Turn Panic into Power, Anxiety into Adrenaline 79

Chapter 11. What Is IRAC? 91

Chapter 12. Daily Habits 113

Chapter 13. Exams 119

Chapter 14. Second Semester, Work on Improving from First Semester 143

Chapter 15. Draft Your Law School Success Plan 159

Chapter 16. Thinking Ahead to After 1L 165

Conclusion 169

Glossary of Law School Terms 171

Excerpt from Author Berman's *Step-by-Step Guide to Contracts* 191

INDEX 193

1L SUCCESS: BECOMING A LAWYER

A Professional Identity Formation Workbook

CHAPTER 1

BEFORE LAW SCHOOL— AND ORIENTATION

Many people will tell you there is nothing special to do to prepare before law school begins. Just take a break so you can relax a bit if you are going straight from college or working in an intense job. Then, show up and be present at Orientation and take it from there.

That can work. But especially if you are first gen or don't know any lawyers, you may want to demystify law school and prepare ahead of time. There are online pre-law programs and books you might read before Orientation or soon after starting law school including:

- *1L of a Ride: A Well-Traveled Professor's Roadmap to Success in the First Year of Law School* (4th Ed.) by Andrew J. McClurg

- *Introduction to the Study and Practice of Law in a Nutshell* (8th Ed.) by Kenney Hegland

- *Cracking the Case Method: Legal Analysis for Law School Success* (3d Ed.) by Paul Bergman, Patrick Goodman, and Thomas Holm

You may complete parts of an online program or read certain chapters of a book—perhaps the ones that make sense to you now—and return to other parts later. Read the parts that inform, prepare, and/or demystify law school, especially if that makes you feel less stress. If these make you feel further stress, save them for later.

In addition to learning about law school, take care of "life logistics" before you start. Find a place to live, explore transportation options, handle student loan matters, create a budget, buy supplies including a new laptop if you need one. Do anything that might clear your plate of outside responsibilities. You want to free up as much time and mental space as possible for the first couple of months of law school.

Another thing some of my students have said was helpful before law school was to take an online typing course to improve their speed and accuracy. This will help with both taking notes in class and typing under pressure on exams.

However you prepare, and even if you've been to campus before, Orientation may feel like you have walked into another world. That is normal.

Law schools put a lot of thought, time, and energy into Orientation. Read anything your school sends about Orientation. This may include homework, such as a case to read and brief (summarize in a particular way that you will learn about), and logistical information such as where to park.

If you have questions or are concerned about something, reach out and ask before you arrive. Some students need clarification about what to wear or how early the building opens if they must arrive before the sessions begin. (Tip: you will likely be given a tour of the building and possibly the campus so wear or bring walking shoes.)

At Orientation, you will hear from key administrators and professors. You may have a mock class and/or a workshop on basic law school skills such as case briefing, note-taking, and outlining. You may attend social events or be asked to participate in a team-building exercise to meet and get to know your future classmates.

The advice in these first sessions will help you succeed every step of the way. But taking in all the information can be totally overwhelming. First, it's often way more than you can absorb. Second, because it's all new, you may not grasp the importance of what is said. Finally, most people are nervous—and nerves can hinder one's ability to take it all in.

In fact, some students find themselves in full panic mode at Orientation. If this is you, you are not alone. Here are some of the stressful internal dialogues students have told me they had in their heads during Orientation, and my responses:

- ***It feels like all of these people are smarter than me. Are they?*** The answer to this one is simple: *No.*

BEFORE LAW SCHOOL—AND ORIENTATION

- ***Will I do as well here as I did in college?*** This is a maybe. Most law schools have forced grading curves so not everyone gets the A. But don't focus on this now. You may have felt similarly nervous on day 1 of high school or college, but you got through those, and you will get through this. Just try to absorb and take notes on anything that seems important and look back at these notes a few weeks into the semester.

- ***Will I be humiliated in class?*** Maybe. Law professors often conduct class in a Q & A format, as opposed to lecturing. Some professors let students know when they will be called on to speak in class; others engage in what is sometimes described as "cold calling" and randomly question students.

    And law professor questions are often not straightforward. Rather, a professor might describe a fictional scenario (called a "hypo") and ask individual students to indicate what the outcome would be and why based on similar court cases read as homework. Sometimes, a student answers in a way the professor expects or likes, so the professor moves on to another question or another student, and that's the end of it. Other times, a professor may "grill" the student, asking repeated follow-up questions in such a way that there is no right answer, or a professor may say the first student was wrong in what feels like a harsh manner and call on another student.

    So, yes, you will likely be called on in class, and that process may feel humiliating. Know that it is not designed as a personal attack. It is a teaching and learning strategy. Some professors do it just because that's how law school was for them; others believe it is the best way to prepare students for future questioning by tough judges or contentious arguments with opposing counsel.

    Do not take it personally and try not to let it bother you. Class participation points are not common in most first-year courses, and rarely would a 1L student be *graded* on the *quality* of an in-class response so long as they did the reading and are prepared. And most professors (other than in legal writing) grade final exams anonymously. So, what happens in class and on exams is entirely separate.

- ***Will I make friends?*** Quite likely, yes! You may be checking out your future classmates, wondering whom you will or won't like. Remember that this is professional school. Think of your classmates as colleagues. They won't know your grades unless you tell them, but they will recall what you said and did in law school. They will remember whether you showed up on time and followed through with your commitments. If you acted professionally in law school, chances are that classmates will refer clients to you and/or give you leads on coveted job opportunities for decades to come.

- Your professional reputation starts at Orientation. I vividly recall my law school orientation. The Dean greeted us with what started as the familiar refrain, "Look to your right, look to your left." But, instead of ending with, "One of you won't be here after this semester," she declared, "One may be your future law partner."

PIF Reflections:

- What have people told you about law school? Which parts do you think are myth and which reality?

- What are you looking forward to and what are you nervous about?

BEFORE LAW SCHOOL—AND ORIENTATION

- How do you want your classmates to think of you?

_____

_____

- What do you want people to remember ten years from now when they hear your name?

_____

_____

Important Info During Orientation

As you start school and throughout your first year, you will have a million questions about every aspect of your new world including:

- Student loans,
- Buying books and accessing online resources,
- Student health resources (physical and mental health and wellness),
- Housing,
- Attendance policies,
- Commuting,
- Summer jobs after 1L, and
- How to register and what to take as 2L and 3L classes.

Knowing whom to talk with or reach out to when you have a particular question, concern, or challenge makes all the difference. So, despite the nerves and distracting thoughts, pay as close attention as you can during Orientation.

Even if you don't remember everything they say (and you won't!), write down the names, titles, and job areas of the people who speak. Put each person in your contacts, along with one helpful tip they shared. Later, if you need something from the Dean of Students or a particular professor, for example, recalling their advice from Orientation can be a great conversation starter.

The chart below can help to keep track of the names of people in each of the various student-facing offices that present at Orientation. You can create a similar chart on your laptop or put info in notes on your phone. You can also add people who speak at Orientation to your Contacts and include their best tips along with their contact info.

Make a note of any documents that law school administrators or faculty say you should read and know where to find them—such as the Student Handbook.

Orientation Notes

TITLE	NAME/CONTACT	NOTES
Dean of the Law School		
Dean of Students		
Academic Support Faculty		
Financial Aid		
Career Planning and Placement		
Professors		
Law Librarian		
Registrar		
Student Leaders		

Future Classmates		
Notes, thoughts, comments:		

PIF Reflections:

1. What are your top three takeaways from Orientation?

_____

_____

2. Name three people you met.

_____

_____

3. What is something that you are confused about and want to clarify?

_____

_____

_____

CHAPTER 2

START ON A POSITIVE FOOT: YOUR PATH IS NOT PRE-DESTINED

The LSAT, GRE, or undergrad GPA *alone* does not predict your first-year grades. What matters most in law school is 1) learning (the rules of law and the rules of the game), and 2) continuous improvement. These are also the most essential attributes of a successful practicing lawyer—someone who is all about learning and making improvements.

Whatever your admissions test scores and undergrad grades, and whatever your first semester grades if you are reading this book in your second semester of 1L, throw yourself into a *growth mindset*. Believe your abilities *can* develop and will improve, so long as you work at it and make necessary adjustments. Commit to continuous improvement throughout law school and beyond.

Let's look at some examples to illustrate fixed mindsets versus growth mindsets:

- A **fixed mindset** would say: "I got a bad grade on my Contracts midterm, [or totally failed that Contracts practice test] so I'm *never* going to understand contracts."
- By contrast, a **growth mindset** says: "I am going to figure out what I didn't understand on that midterm [or practice test] and learn what I don't yet know so I can get higher scores on finals."
- A **fixed mindset** would say: "I got humiliated in Property when I was called on. I'm never going to feel like I belong in law school."
- A **growth mindset** says: "Being called on in class is entirely disconnected from grades. What if

anything can I *learn* from that classroom experience, without letting it affect my confidence?"

Adopting a growth mindset takes intentional work but it helps to stay strong in the face of challenges. It helps you own your power, and succeed. Looking back on previous challenges, we usually learn something valuable from them. So, a primary mission of this workbook is to guide you through a variety of reflections to frame the 1L experience as an opportunity to build confidence, skills, and knowledge, and break free of detracting or negative voices.

This is *not* about quick fixes. It is about cultivating a deeply felt *trust* that you will succeed because you work hard and sensibly, and because you remain doggedly motivated, face challenges and find positive paths forward, and do not ignore the tough parts. You learn from every bump in the road.

Another key part of this process focuses on well-being—physical and mental. This includes developing tools to work effectively when you are working, and rest and recharge when you are not working. We will also address ways to avoid ruminating and worrying—natural tendencies but often traps that steal our precious time and drag us down.

Many students figure out 1L hacks through a lot of trial and error (pun intended), tripping and falling then learning from mistakes. Mistakes are great teachers. And, no matter what happens, you too will make them. Try to reframe *mistakes* as *opportunities*.

But rather than going it alone, find a helpful mentor, maybe a favorite professor or 2L or 3L in an interesting student org. Some schools have TAs or Fellows dedicated to helping 1Ls. Finding a person, even one person, who has been in your shoes can sometimes cut through a whole lot of "noise" and steer you in a positive direction or get you back on track if you're off course.

Books and online resources from reputable publishers can also provide help to put action plans into place. Talk with your law librarians and Academic Support faculty for suggestions.

The key if possible is to try to make positive changes regularly throughout the semester *before* final exams. And, if

START ON A POSITIVE FOOT: YOUR PATH IS NOT PRE-DESTINED

you are reading this book in your second semester, make the changes now, before your next set of final exams.

A critical point, while we are on the topic of finals: grades do not define you. It may not feel like it at the time, but low grades can be gifts. Instead of letting you cruise along believing you are really "getting it," a low grade stops you in your tracks and forces you to figure out how to improve.

You will do your best to prepare and do as well as you can. But try to decide right now that *if* you get a lower grade on a practice test, midterm, or final you will think of it as an invitation to make changes going forward. (How much better does an "invitation" sound than a "failure." Right?!!)

And quick detour to "worst case scenario" land. Imagine 1L grades are posted and you didn't do as well as you would have liked. This too is OK! Unless your grades were so low that you are dismissed, you will be fine. The only opportunities you may "lose" out on are big law firm summer associate gigs (between 1L and 2L) or law review. But there are many other summer jobs that you can get by working closely with your office of career services. And there are many law school activities you can participate in, including moot court, student orgs, or other journals, if that is an experience you want. And some law schools will allow even students with lower GPAs to "write on" to law review.

You've heard the expression, "Turn lemons into lemonade." A number of my former 3L students have actually used lower 1L grades *and their track record of subsequent improvement* as talking points when interviewing for post-graduation law jobs. They powerfully and credibly asserted that precisely because of their resilience, grit, *and ability to learn from mistakes,* they would make excellent lawyers. They promised to fight for their clients with the same energy and commitment demonstrated in making improvements during law school. And they landed great jobs.

So long as your law school GPA improves significantly between 1L and graduation, you have a good chance of passing your first bar exam and going on to have a thriving career. (The title of a recent study published by AccessLex, *"It's not where you start, it's where you finish,"* proves this!)

Take a moment to think about your priorities as you begin law school. You will want to return to this as you work to succeed throughout law school and reflect on who you are becoming as a future lawyer.

PIF: Priorities Reflection

Put a **T** next to every **true** statement and an **F** next to every **false** statement.

___ Studying is my number-one priority. (If this is not true, where does it fall on your priority list?)

___ I am actively taking steps to improve my lifestyle or maintain an already healthy one through exercise, nutrition, and other physical and mental self-care.

___ I usually get a good night's sleep. Or I am taking steps to practice good sleep hygiene.

___ I am willing to look at sample law school exams because I know they will differ from exams I've taken in previous academic experiences.

___ I'm working on improving or maintaining effective time management.

___ I'm actively combating distractions and working to build my concentration.

___ I plan to participate in extracurricular activities only if I have time for them.

___ I am selective about extra responsibilities to which I commit.

___ **TOTAL Ts** ___ **TOTAL Fs**

Hopefully you have far more Ts than Fs. If not, ask if there is anything you might change or adapt—and return to this throughout 1L to see if any of your priorities shift.

START ON A POSITIVE FOOT: YOUR PATH IS NOT PRE-DESTINED

CCC Reflection:

1. How much anxiety or pressure, if any, do you feel because of expectations of your family and community?

2. Do you feel like you belong in law school? If not, why not?

3. What are two things that would make you feel part of your law school?

Hint: when you meet lawyers or upper division law students, ask them what they did during 1L (or what they wish they had done during 1L) that made them feel more a part of their law school community.

Mentors

A mentor is a trusted person who advises and serves by example. Mentors can be beneficial in law school, bar exam preparation after graduation, and for career coaching. Mentors are important for everyone, especially first-generation law students. A law school mentor can:

- Serve as proof that law school is doable so you believe *unequivocally* that you too can not only survive but thrive;
- Discuss your study schedule, and give you tips;
- Check in periodically, especially before finals, to see that you are on target;
- Provide moral support to stay focused and not be bothered by those who don't understand when you need to say No to social invitations and hibernate to study;

- Be a friendly face who "gets it," someone who just pats you on the back and says, "Stick with this. You can do it!"

Look for a mentor who is empathetic and smart, possibly someone with whom you have something in common. Notice I said find *someone*. All you need is one person. Justice Sotomayor in her autobiography, tells how she approached the smartest girl in her class for advice when she wanted to improve in grade school.

If the first person you ask is not someone you click with, try again. And keep trying. It may be hard to find people you connect with, but it will be worth the effort when you do. Having just one close friend, study partner, or mentor can make all the difference in your law school day-to-day.

Sometimes an experienced lawyer or recent graduate can be a good fit. It can help when a recent graduate tells you, "I did it, and you can, too. I had your same professors and same books and I struggled too, but I made it."

You may want a mentor who has been through the same or similar life circumstances. For example, you may want someone who became a parent during law school or someone who worked through law school.

Your family and friends, even if they are supportive, are typically *not* great law school mentors unless they themselves went to law school. A supportive professor can be a fine mentor, as can a lawyer in the community or alumnus of your law school.

Note: Do not rely on your mentor to help you learn the law. Do that work with your school's ASP faculty or a professor, T.A., or peer tutoring program. Your mentor is a coach, someone who will keep you on target. A mentor can help hold you accountable. Good mentors will help their mentees to believe in themselves.

START ON A POSITIVE FOOT: YOUR PATH IS NOT PRE-DESTINED

Potential Mentors

List names of people who might make good mentors or contacts who might suggest good mentors. If you don't know where to start, ask for help identifying prospective mentors from your Dean of Students or Dean of Career Services, ASP faculty, a professor you feel comfortable with, or a faculty advisor to an organization you belong to or are thinking about joining.

_____
_____
_____
_____

CHAPTER 3

BECOME A CRITICAL READER

If asked to identify one factor as the most important to law school success, I would say without hesitation: critical reading.

Let me repeat—*if* there were a law school "magic bullet," it would be to master the skill of close, careful, thoughtful reading.

I use the word *skill* intentionally. Critical reading is not an art or innate talent. It is not like painting a Picasso (which could *only* be done by Picasso!). It is a skill that law students can develop. Yet legal educators rarely teach or even take the time to focus on precision reading in law school.

In a recent law school classroom visit, I watched one of the nation's most prestigious law professors require every student to pull out the Federal Rules of Civil Procedure and parse through a statute, out loud, reading the text word for word. It took almost 30 minutes just to get through the one-sentence rule. I have observed many law school classes and rarely seen anything like that. Yet such detailed reading is the currency of lawyers.

And critical reading is even more important in our busy world of skimming and scrolling! So, whether your professors focus on reading in class or expect you to already be a critical reader, work yourself, from day 1 of law school, to train, get into, and remain committed to good reading habits. The following top ten tips may help as a starting place.

1. Be awake and present (focused not distracted) when you read.
2. Read in a well-lit area.
3. Put your phone in your backpack, in another room, or at least turned face down, and if you are reading on your laptop disable notifications. (If you must keep your phone out to receive emergency calls, arrange your settings so those are your only calls.)

4. Check the table or summary of contents of your casebook and your syllabus to see where each reading fits in context within the course as a whole.
5. Circle the words *"and"* and *"or"* or put a box around them.
6. Underline key terms or highlight sparingly.
7. Write your own thoughts, reactions, and opinions in the margins as you read. Use a pencil if reading printed books; use a stylus if reading online or e-books.
8. Read aloud (under your breath if you are in public), touching words as you read them—especially where concepts are confusing.
9. Look up words in a legal dictionary that you do not know or sense have different meanings in "Legalese."
10. Reread passages you don't understand. If you are still confused, read about the area of law in a hornbook or supplement, then return to the casebook. If you are still confused talk with your professor, ASP faculty, or a TA.

Take a moment now to reflect on your own reading habits.

PIF: Active Reader Reflection

Read the statements below and place a T for true or an F for false in front of each. Read these again two months into law school and at the end of your first semester or beginning of second semester. Ask yourself if any of your reading habits have changed—or if they should change—and why. What does it mean to you to read like a lawyer?

___ I read the Table of Contents or Summary of Contents before I read assigned cases to see where they fit into the course as a whole.

___ I consult hornbook passages about assigned cases I don't understand or to help put the caselaw into context within the subject.

___ I brief cases myself rather than relying on commercial briefs.

___ I build my course outlines on an ongoing basis as we progress through the material.

BECOME A CRITICAL READER 19

___ I write my own course outlines rather than (or in addition to) studying from commercial outlines.

___ I try to restate case holdings in my own words.

___ I look up words I don't understand.

___ I am in a study group or have a study buddy, and we explain rules and concepts to each other.

___ I have found that I study more effectively alone, so that is what I do.

___ I have tried to explain what I'm learning in my law school reading to friends and family who are not lawyers.

___ I read the notes and questions following cases in the casebook, and try to answer them.

___ I diagram the scene or relationships of the parties in cases as I am reading.

___ I write notes and thoughts in the margins of my casebook (reacting to what I agree or disagree with); I don't just "highlight."

___ I keep track of points I do not understand so I can return and figure them out.

___ I read the dissents as well as the majority opinions.

___ I write flash cards with the holdings of cases and definitions of key terms, if I am going to have closed book final exams.

___ I listen carefully in class and think about what I understood differently from the reading I did before class. I continue to think after class.

___ I take notes in class and organize them soon after class into a rough draft course outline.

One of my favorite law professors told our first-year section to write in our casebooks as we read, noting our thoughts and reactions to the decisions. (*"What was this judge thinking?!"*) Why would my professor suggest that, especially when students are nearly always instructed *not* to write their own personal opinions on exams? Someday we would find our 1L notes fascinating, my professor said, and the books would be valuable if we ever became famous. (He mentioned that an annotated casebook from a former US Supreme Court Justice had just fetched a large sum of money.) Looking back, I suspect his real motive was simply to keep us actively engaged in the material. It worked.

Reading or Writing Challenges

If you aren't confident that you are understanding the reading you are required to complete, or that you can produce grammatically correct, clearly written sentences and paragraphs, practice reading as much as possible.

Reading and writing are skills, not talents; the more we practice them the better we become. And they are intertwined; reading a lot typically makes someone a stronger writer and vice versa.

In addition to your own daily practice, seek help from a reliable resource. Often there are writing centers at the law school or on the main campus if you are part of a university. There also many English as a New Language (ENL) resources, if those would be helpful. (Note: this used to be referred to as "ESL, English as a Second Language" so you might try that as a search term.)

Remember to be kind to yourself and don't expect this part to be easy. Even if you thought you read a lot and read and wrote well in college, law school reading and writing may be different, and for many students, harder.

For students who are unfamiliar with legal terminology or want basic information on the American court system and other foundational knowledge, all of which can help enhance critical reading, here are some resources:

1. https://www.Civics101Podcast.org
2. https://www.iCivics.org
3. Khan Academy, https://www.khanacademy.org
4. Legal English Resources page on Georgetown Legal English Blog—designed for non-English speakers with resources that useful for all new law students.
5. Nolo.com including <u>Represent Yourself in Court</u> and <u>The Criminal Law Handbook</u>, books I co-authored that are designed for non-lawyers and that law students find to be clear, approachable overviews of civil and criminal court procedures.

Testing Accommodations

If you know you need or think that you may need accommodations for a disability, talk to your law school and/or university's disability officer, Dean of Students, or ASP faculty. And, looking ahead, if you might need accommodations for the bar exam after graduation, it may be important to lay this foundation early, throughout law school, so make an appointment this 1L year with the person at your school who is in charge of disability accommodations.

Think While You Read

Law school reading is not just letting our eyes roll around the screen as we do when we scroll social media. Effective law school reading requires being tuned in and thinking while you take in words, sentences, and paragraphs.

When we look at websites or social media, our eyes tend to dart about the screen. We check out something at the top, then pop to the middle or bottom, then go back up top. For law school reading, whether online or on paper, especially as you begin 1L, slow down. Try to read full sentences from left to right and full pages, from top to bottom. Breathe while you read. Pretend you have all the time in the world.

I know you don't have all the time in the world and that you are probably super stressed about time. But by acting *as if* you have time, you may absorb more and have better comprehension than you would if you are constantly looking at the clock or your phone for the time. (As noted above, keep your phone away while reading cases.)

At first the reading will be very slow and it's easy to get impatient—or down on yourself that it's taking so long. But, if you keep at it, your vocabulary will increase geometrically, as will your comprehension and speed.

Don't be surprised if your head hurts when reading your casebook. And don't assume you'll "get it" easily or quickly. Simple cases that you understand right away are gifts. You may need to stop to look up terms, take notes, think further, ask yourself what particular sentences mean and why they are important, think more, read the author's notes and/or a hornbook passage (or summary from a reliable supplement) that relates to the rules or policies discussed in the case, then read the case yet again. There is nothing wrong with you. It is supposed to be hard!

That said, don't spend hours just re-reading the same words and hoping it will get easier. If you feel stuck, consult a reliable outside resources (hornbook or supplement), then go back to the case with some context.

> **PIF Reflections:**
>
> - Describe your thinking process when reading law school cases. What are you looking for and why? What points are your professors stressing and is each professor emphasizing the same parts of the cases? (Likely some will have more interest in procedural history, for example, while others will focus on facts, holding, and reasoning in the instant case only.)
>
> - What interests you, what is frustrating, and why?
>
> - What is an example of something you read and did not understand? What did you do about that?
>
> - Do you think that when you are a lawyer you will understand everything you read right away?

In a lot of our education and personal reading prior to law school, we skimmed over things we didn't understand—hoping for "context clues" or just thinking the details may not be that important. The key was to get the "gist."

BECOME A CRITICAL READER 23

Law school changes this. Details are critical. The liability (civil) or guilt (criminal) of future clients may turn on one word, or the placement of one comma. It is essential to know the precise meaning of words.

Words are the tools of our trade as lawyers. Words are our currency. We use words to earn a living. Expect to develop different reading habits. But don't expect this to happen overnight. Work at it.

Try not to get discouraged; becoming skilled at law school reading will take time. But keep at it every day and your reading will become a power tool.

If you want to test yourself, turn to the Glossary toward the back of this book and see how many words you already know. Try to use them each accurately in a sentence. Then, explain their meaning in plain English as if you were speaking to a non-lawyer client.

There are many helpful resources for law students seeking additional training in critical reading, including: *Critical Reading for Success in Law School and Beyond* (2d ed. West Academic) by Jane Grise, and *Cracking the Case Method: Legal Analysis for Law School Success* (3d ed. West Academic) by Paul Bergman, Patrick Goodman, and Thomas Holm.

CHAPTER 4

FIND YOUR WHY

Depending on when you are reading this, it may feel like a lifetime ago when you drafted your law school admissions essays. What did you write? What were you thinking about? Did you want to give a voice to people who can't or don't know how to defend themselves? Did you want power, credibility, and/or to avoid feeling vulnerable? Did you seek the ability to earn a good living for yourself and your family? Who or what inspires you?

It helps to return from time to time to the reasons that drew you in and propelled you to invest the time, energy, money, and effort to get your J.D., especially on long study days when you are tired.

Keeping your dreams in mind will help keep the motivation fire lit! In one January class, a student told me, "Yesterday was Martin Luther King's birthday—a day that reminds me every year why I went to law school. I see this man, standing between the Washington Monument and Lincoln Memorial; I hear the words with which he transfixed the world. I wanted a law license to continue to help make that dream a reality."

It is easy in all the stress of starting and surviving in law school to disconnect from our vision. We must sometimes take affirmative, intentional steps to reconnect.

I am reminded of another vision, this one from a law school graduate who passionately described several superheroes and what she admired about each of them. Some, such as Superman and Spiderman, had impressive magical powers. But, she was most inspired by Batman—a guy who achieved amazing feats *without* supernatural powers. What makes Batman, *a distinctly human individual,* so strong? His knowledge and his power tools! She spoke of the power of her legal education and of wearing her law license like a "tool belt." She felt this awesome force rise in her each time she rose in court to speak on a client's behalf.

Some people go to law school to fulfill a parent or grandparent's dream. If that is you, don't make that "less than" in your mind. Think about how proud you are making that person. And know that you will forge your own path at the same time as your accomplishments bring joy to someone you love; you are earning a degree that brings both opportunity and flexibility.

What if you really had no "good reasons" to go to law school? Let's say it was purely a default choice—you weren't interested in business or medicine, so it seemed like the best option for grad school—something you felt you had to do. All good! I still want you to identify your *why*.

Do it now. Look around. Find at least one lawyer or legal organization you admire. Consider people who were trained as lawyers and are not practicing, entrepreneurs, politicians, or people who serve on boards of directors of corporations or nonprofits. Look at lawyers who speak for people who cannot or who solve thorny problems. If there's no one today, look at a historical figure who was a lawyer. Identify at least one person who was trained as a lawyer with qualities you respect or professional opportunities you seek.

You may scoff at this discussion of dreams. You came to law school to find a job that would pay the bills and repay your student loans. That's a great reason and a serious motivator! Write it in the Reflection below.

Whatever motivates you, just identifying a "why," *naming it*, will help you succeed in law school. Holding onto your sense of purpose will help you to pass the bar exam and find meaningful work after you graduate.

It's a bit like tennis; your eyes must focus first on where the ball is coming from and then on where you want it to go with your stroke and follow-through. Here too you may need to first look briefly back to why you decided to pursue a legal education so you can look confidently toward where you are heading.

Now, where you end up working may be very different from what you see today as your vision. That too is just fine. You and most people in your class will likely end up changing jobs many times throughout your career. That's great. Your "why" isn't a rigid "must do"—it's an inspiring force that leads you forward.

FIND YOUR WHY

With a "why" it is easier to combat day-to-day frustrations. Without a "why," law school and its intense challenges can feel like moving through a dark, endless tunnel. Just being driven and inspired by a *why* (even if your *why* changes) helps you see the light at the end of the tunnel, shining brightly on a hopeful future after you are licensed. This in turn will help you keep moving, taking steps forward, and doing the necessary follow-through to realize your full potential.

> **PIF Reflection: Why Law School?**
>
> Take a moment and write out why you chose law school? (Note: try answering this without looking at what you wrote in the Introduction; then, check back and see if you responded differently.)
>
> _____
> _____
> _____
>
> Then jot down a few thoughts on what power a law license will give you. (The power to earn a living and support yourself and your family? The power to effect positive change, help people, and make the world a better place?)
>
> _____
> _____
> _____

You might be thinking, '*Really?? All this positivity and optimism is ridiculous. With climate change and AI, I have real doubts that I'll even have a professional future to look forward to.*'

If you have worry and doubts, you are in good company and have good cause for concern about the future. It can be difficult in our uncertain times even to hold onto the basic belief that you are pursuing something worthwhile. But, to put in the work necessary for long-term success, you need sustainable, rechargeable fuel. Inspiration and motivation in a growth mindset provide powerful renewable intellectual and emotional "fuel" reserves.

And despite all of society's challenges, there is very good reason to have faith that you are working to earn a lifetime license that will bring many different job opportunities, over decades. You are training to think critically and to problem solve. Those are skills that will keep you nimble.

You are learning how to learn. When laws, rules, policies, and technology change, and they will many times throughout your career, you will know how to adapt. Embrace the fact that your professional road is paved with continuous learning and continuous improvement.

Even when things were relatively "stable" in the "outside world," the legal profession demanded adaptability. You can never know it all. Lawyers must learn a host of new facts and rules with every new client.

It may be precisely *because of your legal education* that you are well-positioned to embrace and not fear change. And, consider this: you, *unique you, with your legal training*, may be part of the solution that makes the future better for all of us.

I'm not saying it won't be hard to remain hopeful on certain days. I'm saying it is logical and right to believe you will have a future because you will adapt and thrive. I am saying that to realize the success you deserve, you must have faith in tomorrow, and faith in yourself.

"Adapt or perish, now as ever, is nature's inexorable imperative."

—H. G. WELLS—

CHAPTER 5

HARD WORK IS THE MOST IMPORTANT PART OF SUCCESS

The cornerstone of successful law study, law practice, and being a successful professional is and always will be *hard work*.

"Patience and perseverance have a magical effect before which difficulties disappear and obstacles vanish."

—JOHN QUINCY ADAMS—

Perhaps it is human nature to seek the easy route. On popular lawyer shows, the attorney always wins the case—and typically does so in about 30 minutes. Some commercial study aids promise to make law school easy with short lectures, apps, and games.

I have nothing against fun in studying or in life. I am all for it. But I do not believe that fun and hard work are mutually exclusive. And I remain steadfastly convinced that working slowly, steadily, carefully, and *hard* is essential for sustained success, especially in law.

Persistence and attention to detail may not be glamorous, but they are necessary. Succeed slowly, and you will go far. Rush, and you may produce sloppy work. There are no shortcuts.

During final exams, you will have to be "on," performing at peak levels for the length of the exam (often 2–3 hours or more). Does it make sense to "train" in short spurts with frequent breaks, chilling and just *hoping* you'll do well? No!

How many people train for a marathon by sitting in a comfy chair reading articles about running, taking multiple coffee breaks, and *hoping* they'll nail the race? Not many.

Think about it from another perspective. Let's say *you* or a close family member were falsely accused of a crime and needed legal counsel. Would you want a lawyer willing to work as hard as needed to give you the best defense, or would you want someone looking for shortcuts?

> **"The harder I work, the luckier I get."**
> —SAM GOLDWYN—

I frequently hear complaints from stressed-out students about not having time to do it all. I get it! Time is our most precious resource, and it is finite.

We'll talk about time management soon, but before we do, let me suggest thinking about the whole concept as *protecting time* rather than managing time.

How does that sound? As a professional, you will be someone who is paid for your expertise and your time. Think about how valuable your time really is.

Also, sometimes we confuse how much time something takes with how challenging it is. Remember, law school is supposed to be hard, and it should take time. You will soon be responsible for other people's lives and livelihoods. And I suspect that you would not have chosen law if deep down you really wanted things to be easy.

But we have all come to expect *quick* solutions—and too often we get down on ourselves when things don't come quickly *and* easily—especially for those of us who have achieved in the past academically.

We expect to find every answer in a moment's Internet search. We are told that instructional videos should be no more than a few minutes in length. But the legal doctrine, procedures, and skills you must learn and the analysis you will be expected to perform are parts of a system developed when the world moved more slowly. Just because information may be available any time of day or night, at the touch of a finger, does not mean that information is easy to understand.

HARD WORK IS THE MOST IMPORTANT
PART OF SUCCESS

And, even if you read and understand concepts quickly, it takes training to learn to communicate a logical, thorough, reasoned analysis of legal issues to someone else. So be kind to yourself if everything, including your daily reading, takes more time that you think it "should."

Hard work in law school requires being focused, turning away from the endless temptations of our instant-gratification society and toward developing the patience necessary to acquire a command of legal knowledge and skills required to do well on exams. Patient persistence is a pillar of professional success. (Apparently, I am fond of "P" alliterations.)

Law school, although it may require some memorized knowledge, is not about regurgitating facts. It is about logical *reasoning*. It is about seeing how rules and principles apply to new facts, and figuring out *why* a particular outcome should or should not result in each new situation.

Remember what I said earlier about adaptability? Every client will have a new situation even if they are coming to you about an area of law you are familiar with. So, there may be new things to learn and research in every new case.

And, in the "real world," you will wish that *all* you had to deal with were facts, rules, and logic! People's lives and legal problems are riddled with emotion and passion. You may work with opposing counsel, colleagues, or even decision makers whose concerns are not about following the rules, fairness, or justice, but about revenge or self-promotion. They may exhibit displaced anger. (Picture the person who is angry at the boss but kicks the dog.) Such issues pose far more difficult challenges than law school because they are irrational.

Do not expect the hard work to end after 1L or after graduation. Your days will be filled with challenge, so make peace with hard work starting today; learn to embrace challenge and delight in victories that come after the sweat and tears. Do not think that something is wrong with you because you have to work hard.

When in doubt, in law and in life, always and at every turn, get back to work. Hard work is not punishment. Seasoned with a bit of luck, hard work is the key ingredient to success. And you will be happier if you see your work as worthwhile and rewarding, and realize how fortunate you are to be able to pursue an academic or professional goal.

Do not waste one moment feeling bitter or angry or annoyed that you *have to* study. You *get* to study! It truly is a privilege. Change any perspective you may have to the contrary. Consider the daily work struggles of manual laborers or the far too many people fighting to survive war, hunger, and homelessness. Recognize the gift that it is to be able to spend time studying.

I always knew and believed that the privilege of studying was a gift, but I felt particular gratitude when I worked at a law school in South Florida. As I drove onto campus, stunned by the beauty of manicured green lawns and palm trees, I saw and so appreciated the landscaping staff, covered head to toe because of mosquito-transmitted diseases, on what was an oppressively hot and humid day. Drenched in sweat after the minute walk from an air-conditioned car to an air-conditioned building, I thought about everyone working outdoors. I frequently shared this perspective, and together many of us were reminded of how comfortable we were working and studying in that building. We quickly saw the "glass" not just "half full" but truly overflowing.

Hard work *does* mean that you:

- Stay limber in mind and spirit—keep learning new things and staying at the top of your game.
- Exercise, eat healthy foods, and get sufficient sleep. All of these feed your brain, the organ you need to study productively. So if you think there is no time for these, think again. Studying when you have slept well is almost always far more productive than studying when you are exhausted.)
- Laugh and smile while you study. Studying is *not* torture. It's hard work. And it will be a huge accomplishment when you graduate and pass the bar. You are doing this (law school) because you *want* to. It is a privilege to be able to dedicate the time and effort to achieve your goals.

HARD WORK IS THE MOST IMPORTANT PART OF SUCCESS 33

- Seek help to continuously learn how to work smarter and more strategically, and accept assistance from trustworthy resources that can help you improve.

Hard work does **not** mean that you should:

- Work to the point of exhaustion.
- Think it frivolous to take time off from work for exercise. (Movement will make you more productive.)
- Hate it all but push on because you must.
- Repeat the same mistakes continuously without seeking help because "it's supposed to be hard."

PIF Reflection:

What does "hard work" mean to me?

_____
_____
_____

List 2 memories of or examples of when "hard work" was fun for you, and two where such work was frustrating. What differed in those experiences?

_____
_____
_____

As part of my commitment to hard work, for the remainder of the semester, I want to make sure that I **do**:

_____
_____
_____

As part of my commitment to hard work, for the remainder of the semester, I want to make sure that I **do not**:

_____
_____
_____

CHAPTER 6

VISUALIZE YOURSELF AS A LAWYER

Some big goals are easier to realize if you picture yourself already there and work backward.

Take a moment with me now to *practice* introducing yourself as a lawyer. I know that may sound silly, but just saying the words and seeing yourself in the future can be transformative.

Go ahead. Stand in front of a mirror and privately say the following: "Hello, my name is _____. I am an attorney licensed here in [your jurisdiction]." Repeat it a few times.

You can also do this with others, in a class or workshop. Pair up and picture yourselves meeting at a bar association event or networking at a cocktail hour before a conference. Include in your introductions, "I'm pleased to meet you" and some facts about yourself—your "elevator pitch."

Switch partners several times so you can practice not only with the words but getting comfortable saying them. *Being a lawyer is not just what you are doing, but who you are becoming.*

By second semester, you'll not only want to have "tried on" saying the words in this sort of an introduction exercise, you might want to join a local bar association as a student member or the ABA Student Lawyer section. You might take one morning to stop by a local courthouse, walk the halls, and imagine yourself as one of the "suits" rushing around with your briefcase. This can be helpful especially if you do not come from a family of lawyers. If your mom or dad is a lawyer, it is easier to see yourself that way. But if you don't have any close role models in the legal profession, get into a courthouse at some point during law school.

Sit and observe a courtroom proceeding. Is there anything you don't understand or *couldn't* understand by asking questions? If time permits, approach the bailiff and very respectfully say that you are a law student there to observe and learn from the proceedings, and ask if the judge might have time to meet with you for a minute or two. You would be surprised how many judges might invite you into chambers and share their wisdom, perspectives, and advice for you as a future lawyer. (If you get in, send that judge a thank you note and stay in touch!)

> **CCC/PIF Reflection:**
>
> 1. Name a lawyer (living or historical) who shares one of your identities.
>
> _____
> _____
> _____
>
> 2. List at least two challenges that lawyer faced.
>
> _____
> _____
> _____
>
> 3. What qualities do you have that will make you sensitive to the needs of future clients?
>
> _____
> _____
> _____

Second semester or during your 2L year, you might also want to meet some lawyers, and maybe ask them for "informational interviews." (This is not the time to ask for a job; it's just to learn about the work they do.) Lawyers love to talk about their work, especially when you are asking nothing in return. Some may even offer to let you "shadow" them for a day or show you the courthouse.

> **PIF Exercise:**
>
> Write a brief email to a lawyer in your community asking to talk. It doesn't have to be a real lawyer, just call them "Attorney X." Don't send it. Just keep it in your "drafts" folder. It's the act of writing that is important now. I want you to see the language you use to describe yourself and why you are

VISUALIZE YOURSELF AS A LAWYER

interested in meeting this person. Eventually, in second semester or 2L when you decide to contact someone specific, you might return to this language. For now, just see how it feels to contact a lawyer you might connect with.

PIF Reflection: Who will I be as a lawyer?

How would you describe yourself as a lawyer? How would you want others to describe you?

_____
_____
_____

If you or a close family member had a legal problem, what qualities would you want in the lawyer you hire to represent you or your family?

_____
_____
_____

I know if I needed a lawyer, I would want someone *thoughtful, who listens and reasons well, and reads carefully—someone who is detail oriented, keeps their word, and has earned the respect of colleagues and clients alike.* Anything you would add about how you see yourself as a professional and how you want to be seen by others?

_____
_____
_____

CHAPTER 7

ENHANCE FOCUS, REDUCE DISTRACTIONS

This 1L year will require focus and discipline—likely at a different level than you are used to. You'll want to reduce distractions throughout the semester and eliminate them during exam periods. You want to work toward a situation where you control what distractions you let in and when.

Because distractions steal your time, distraction management is a corollary of time management.

To effectively manage time, you must first know how you spend your time. Then, you can be in control. The reflection work you will complete in this chapter will help you see how much time things really take. We'll also look at the order in which you complete tasks and how that may enhance learning. For example, it may be more productive (and ultimately save time) to complete certain readings and begin a draft outline before class or right after class than to wait until the weekend or end of the semester.

> **PIF Reflection: Weekly Time Allocations**
>
> Before we get too deeply into protecting time and managing distractions, and before you think a lot, take 3–5 minutes and enter the approximate number of hours you spend each week on the following activities/tasks. Don't look anything up in a calendar—just take a typical week, or this current week, and put down some numbers.
>
> **Hours Task/Activity**
>
> ___ Work (include remote and onsite work you do as part of employment)
>
> ___ Non-work-related communications (include texting, audio or video calls)
>
> ___ Family/friends commitments, including meals, celebrations, helping relatives with errands or tasks for which they depend on you. Only log these once, so if you include these in another category below, leave this one blank.

___ Commuting (to work, to school)

___ Exercise

___ Religious observances and/or spiritual practices, including prayer, services, holidays, weddings, bar mitzvahs, christenings, and the like, as well as meditation or any spiritual reflection time.

___ Community, neighborhood, or other volunteer work

___ Childcare, care of elderly or other relatives, pet care (including walking the dog)

___ Sleep

___ Meal prep (include shopping and cooking)

___ Eating meals (be sure to log the time to actually eat and social time around meals)

___ Self-care

___ Health care (include medical care for yourself and others who depend on you)

___ Personal finance and record-keeping

___ Recreation and relaxation—and you may want to subtotal out various types of media you interact with so you capture whatever you do to unwind.

___ Other:

   ___ Subtotal:

___ *Study:*

   ___ Total:

Did your list total more than 168 hours? There are only 168 hours in the week! How much time is allocated for study? Are you actually studying as many hours as you think you are? I intentionally listed study last because people tend to inflate their time spent studying. I want you to see how much time you have left after everything other than study is listed.

Now, try re-ordering your list of weekly time allocations, this time with "study" *first*. What if anything differs when you list study time before anything else? Do you increase its allocated time?

ENHANCE FOCUS, REDUCE DISTRACTIONS 41

> **PIF Reflection: Time List Re-Ordered with Study First**
>
> **Hours Task/Activity**
>
> ___ *Study*
>
> ___ Work
>
> ___ Non-work-related communications
>
> ___ Family/friends
>
> ___ Commuting
>
> ___ Exercise
>
> ___ Religious observances and/or spiritual practices
>
> ___ Community, neighborhood, or other volunteer work.
>
> ___ Childcare, care of elderly or other relatives, pet care
>
> ___ Sleep
>
> ___ Meals (prep and eating) prep
>
> ___ Self-care (including health care)
>
> ___ Personal finance
>
> ___ Recreation and relaxation
>
> ___ Other:
>
> ___ **Total:**

Are you now at/under 168 hours? What if anything do you still need to adjust?

"In reading the lives of great men, I found that the first victory they won was over themselves ... self-discipline with all of them came first."

—HARRY S. TRUMAN—

As I suggested earlier, instead of focusing on "time *management,*" which can feel like a stressful chore, think about *protecting* your time. (Does "protecting your time" sound harder or easier, more or less important?)

Your time is precious, indeed invaluable, and you must work to guard it. We face endless distractions and interruptions, from the external onslaught of invasive texts, alerts, e-mails, and phone calls to the deeply internal distractions of worry and fear.

There are worthwhile distractions (those that nourish and recharge your batteries), there are destructive distractions (soul-crushing disappointments), and there are those in between that are more neutral but nonetheless waste time.

We'll talk together later and work through some reflections that will help combat fears, reduce anxiety, and protect yourself from people who are not positive. Here and now, our goal is just that you become aware of where your time goes. Armed with awareness, you will be able to make empowered decisions about how you choose to spend your time. Awareness will also help you battle the "time thieves" that steal minutes or hours without even noticing.

An example of a sneaky time thief is transition time. You may not be aware of how much time gets wasted when you move between tasks. Unconscious spending of time is like unconscious consumption of calories. (We fail to count the minutes between tasks just like we fail to count snacks between meals. But they add up.)

Another time thief is procrastination. When we avoid doing one thing, we often fill the time with something we don't really value. One way to deal with procrastination is to keep lists of different types of tasks so that you can switch to something else that you nonetheless need or want to do. Sometimes it can help to just change things up, for example doing work that demands different parts of you—some active and others passive, some that require reading and others that require listening. When you are too tired to complete an active task, such as reading and briefing cases or updating your own course outlines and find yourself procrastinating with something unhelpful (for example scrolling on social media and feeling jealous that others are "playing" while you "have to study"), try something less demanding but that nonetheless needs to be done such as managing your finances (reviewing account statements, paying bills), reading law school emails, listening to an uplifting or empowering podcast, or exercising.

Just changing gears and doing a different type of task or switching to study a different subject may allow you to get a "second wind" and accomplish tasks that will move you forward, rather than allowing a time vampire such as mindless TV to sweep in and consume your time.

Now, I'm not criticizing TV. It may be precisely what you need to unwind and re-charge. I'm simply pointing out the difference between deliberate time choices and those that become unintentional defaults.

If you decide to take a TV break, enjoy it. Don't just hit the remote because you feel you can't focus.

If you are tired of working, certain intentional activities may propel you more directly toward your success goals. For example, one great way to take a "productive" study break is to exercise or engage in some form of movement. Time spent keeping your body alert will in turn help your critical thinking.

And, it doesn't have to be an "either/or." You can do both simultaneously. For example, you can listen to recorded lectures, podcasts, or your own voice reading your course outlines while you walk or work out.

Again, the most important thing for now is to know where you are spending time and where you want to be spending time and try to keep those aligned as much as possible—and to be *all in* with whatever you choose to spend your time on.

As part of our next reflection, you will look at each day for at least a week. Starting when you wake up and ending when you go to sleep, log what you do in fifteen-minute increments if you can, as you might bill a client. (In private practice, you might track time in six-minute increments.) This is an effective way to see where your time is being used productively and where it is slipping away. You cannot effectively reduce distractions when you do not know what is distracting you! You can use a simple chart or spreadsheet set up like the samples below.

PIF Reflection: Daily Time Sheets

As an attorney, you will likely track your time. Your time is a professional asset, and it helps to start in law school thinking about your time as very valuable. Complete this chart over the course of a week to see where your time is going. Note that in addition to self-explanatory categories such as day, time, and activity, there are columns for who initiated the activity and whether it is something you want or need to do, or something someone else wants you to do.

Date/Day	Activity	Initiated by	Total Time	Necessity/ Distraction	Notes: Eliminate? Deter? Do at a Different Time? Multitask?
Morning					
Afternoon					
Evening					

ENHANCE FOCUS, REDUCE DISTRACTIONS

Assessment:
- How much of what you do is necessary?
- Is the time of day you complete each task the most productive time for that task?
- How do you feel about "tracking your time"?
- Name three things you learned after tracking your time for a week:

1. _____
2. _____
3. _____

<u>Keep Commitments but Maintain Flexibility</u>

As you schedule time for study and intentional study breaks, work on keeping commitments to yourself—just as you will keep commitments to colleagues and future clients.

You are important. You are worth every ounce of the time, energy, and money you are investing right now in your future.

Try picturing your study time as you would an appointment with an expert physician you have waited months to see. You would not cancel on that doctor unless it were an emergency. Don't cancel on yourself.

Do have a "Plan B" to modify your schedule if necessary. Let's say you calendared 6–10pm to study, but it's an off day and catch yourself zoning out, reading the same paragraph over and over again. What should you do?

First, acknowledge that your mind drifted and try to turn it back to reading. Maybe read a few paragraphs aloud to pull yourself back in. If that doesn't work, get up, stretch, and try again. Sill no luck? Drink some water, or splash the water on your face, then go back to the books. If after these, you still aren't alert enough to learn productively, shift to another subject or a less-active (but necessary) task. If you still can't focus, go to sleep and return to studying the next day—without judging yourself.

In other words, stay committed to your schedule, but not rigidly so. Push yourself, but not if it's counterproductive.

Time spent being critical of yourself is a waste. Push yourself positively, or take healthy breaks (walks, naps, healthy snacks). But don't berate yourself (unless that helps you to be more productive).

If you are a working student, depending on your other commitments, you may be more successful with a target goal of accomplishing certain tasks over several days, especially if you have an unpredictable work schedule. A Monday and Tuesday may be particularly heavy at work, but later in the week things lighten up. So, you may have to finish study tasks that you'd planned to complete at the beginning of the week on a Thursday and Friday. That's fine. Just stay accountable to yourself. Make sure the tasks get done at whatever alternative time you designate.

Variety

Studying in different ways can help to maintain focus and build stamina. Shaking things up can also prevent burnout. For example, try to:

- Talk through concepts with a friend, study buddy, or mentor (perhaps over coffee). The person doesn't need a legal background; explaining legal rules to non-lawyers can help you to better understand them.

- Learn rules by singing them to the melody of a popular tune. (One of my professors set all of civil procedure to music.)

- Make flowcharts or diagrams of areas you are studying.

- Record yourself reading key rules. You will learn both by making the recording and listening to it. (It can have an empowering effect to hear your own voice confidently stating rules.)

ENHANCE FOCUS, REDUCE DISTRACTIONS

PIF Reflection: How to Enjoy Studying

1. List three things that might make studying more fun for you.

   _____

   _____

2. List three things that make studying particularly annoying or difficult (then think about possible changes to either make the experience better or re-frame the difficulties as challenges/opportunities.

   _____

   _____

Studying can be more enjoyable when you vary your study strategies, study in comfortable places, and give yourself rewards. But, even when you add levity, it can still feel like a "daily grind." Stick as much as possible to a schedule. Think of your reading and case-briefing as a daily practice or habit. And, just like any habit, even hard ones like working out, the more consistently you practice them the easier they get.

- Don't expect each day to be miraculous. Expect slow and steady progress.
- Don't spin your wheels. When you hit a wall (and you will!), change gears or take a break.
- Don't be annoyed when you feel discouraged. Be patient and kind with yourself. Each day you are building stamina.
- Don't waste time feeling sorry for yourself that you *have to* study while others play. You *get to* study. And you will get to reap the future rewards of all your hard work.

PIF Reflection: A Look Toward Finals

The reflections above give you a picture of how you spend your time. They hopefully shed light on what feels productive versus what steals or wastes time. Even though finals may be months off, take a moment and think about what you can do to prioritize time for studying during the month before exams? Anything you can eliminate entirely for that month? Anything you can put off until December (or June after 2d semester)?

Here are some ideas:

- I have to read emails from school, but I can turn notifications off and read only during study breaks. And I can temporarily stop social media that isn't necessary or uplifting.
- I have to eat, but I can shave off meal prep time by shopping, cooking, and freezing meals for the week each Sunday evening while listening to audio recordings of class.
- I have to walk the dog, but I can use that time for my own exercise (and to listen to a law podcast or class recording).
- I have to pay bills and answer emails, but that doesn't require the same kind of focus that studying does, so I'll do that later in the day when I'm too tired to study.
- I have to acknowledge birthdays of family and friends, but I will send an e-mail or note that says "rain check to celebrate in December (or May) after finals."

Your turn:

I have to _____, but I can save time by _____.

I have to _____, but I can save time by _____.

I have to _____, but I can save time by _____.

I have to _____, but I can save time by _____.

Think of this as a preview now. Revisit this reflection about 4-6 weeks before finals so you have a plan when you will need to go into "crunch mode."

Control Your Communications and Manage Your Media; Don't Let Them Control You

You can control some distractions by *deciding* not to interrupt yourself or your study flow, such as for texts or emails. You can turn off notifications. It is easy to say, "It's just one text," or "I would have needed a break anyway sooner or later." But even a brief text exchange will break your concentration.

Will you be texting during exams? No. So, decide not to interrupt yourself now, during your study time. (Does it help to call it a study "commitment"?)

Try creating "office hours" for checking messages and social media and schedule these during your least productive study times. That way you control what you let cut into your study, sleep, exercise and other vital time.

E-distractions are particularly insidious because much of your studying is online. If you use e-books or must log on to a learning management system such as Canvas or Blackboard, the very same device you learn on is also luring you away with rabbit holes of temptation. And, unless social media posts provide positive peer pressure or support, they will typically not move you toward success and may be downright destructive if they cause you to take on other people's anxiety. So, you may want to deactivate certain accounts during the semester, especially as you move closer to finals.

PIF Reflection:

Name two ways you think your communication tools or media control you or take away time you need to spend on study or self-care:

1.

2.

List two strategies you might employ to control your messages and media:

1.

2.

Law Students with Children or Other Dependent Care Responsibilities

Many nontraditional students say they feel guilty that law school is taking them away from their kids. If you are a parent and a law student, one way to reframe the pressure that puts on you is to know that your studying is positive role modeling. And, action is often much more effective than preaching, so don't be surprised if your children do better in school when they see you studying. You are teaching them discipline and the value of hard work through your actions.

Think too about the following:

- If you have dependent children or aging parents who must be able to reach you in an emergency, give them a code or special ringtone for an emergency call or text. You'll know if it's something you need to read or listen to right away or if it can wait until you decide to take the study break. Use the "do not disturb" functions; people you favorite can still reach you in an emergency by phoning twice.

- Keep personal "office hours" so your family knows when you are available and when you are studying and not to be interrupted except in emergencies. Designate family time and keep your commitment. Even if family time is an hour dinner every night, sit down together and be entirely present. It is even more important when you are gone a lot to be consistent and reliable. If people know when they can depend on you to give them your full attention, they may be better able to leave you alone the rest of the day.

- Be sure to include your family (children, significant other, parents) in your studying when/if you can productively do so. When you take breaks, ask them to test you with flash cards. (Just be prepared, kids may memorize rules faster than you!)

- Play audio versions of lectures or law podcasts while you are driving, cooking, cleaning, or playing with young children.

- Test yourself with flashcards on your smartphone while at the park or waiting in line at the market.

ENHANCE FOCUS, REDUCE DISTRACTIONS 51

- If you have young children, read or sing your cases or course outlines aloud. Infants and toddlers mostly just want to hear your voice and be close to you. Doesn't matter if reading Dr. Seuss, *Goodnight Moon*, or *Farnsworth on Contracts*!
- Plan something fun for the family after finals.

Reflection for students who are caretakers for or responsible for others:

List three strategies you are willing to try that might better align your study commitments with your other responsibilities?

1.
2.
3.

Money worries can also become time thieves. Finances are totally legit concerns, so if you need help or even just find you are worrying a lot about money, meet with your financial aid office and complete the online materials in MAX by AccessLex, a reputable free course on financial planning for law students. Sometimes, the fear comes from not knowing how you will be able to repay loans or other concerns that can be better managed with more information. When it comes to money, knowledge is power.

PIF Reflection: Time and Money

You must study and you must pay bills/handle financial matters. Do you:

A. Start the day paying bills, then worry about money generally, think about student loans and scroll financial sites only to find yourself an hour later on something that could have been done in two minutes?

B. Study first and pay the bills quickly at the end of a productive day, when you are too tired to read cases and think?

C. Study for a few hours; then take a break to have a snack and pay the bills while eating something, then get back to work?

> D. Put off paying bills until you incur late fees, feel compounded anxiety about money, and lose time with guilt and stress instead of productive studying?
>
> B or C make sense. And, some people are fine quickly handling financial details in the morning and moving on to a productive day, fine. But A and D are traps. Watch out for traps. Control the time of day you handle things you must deal with to maximize productivity.
>
> Again, talk with someone in your financial aid office and work through trustworthy financial planning resources for law students such as those in the free MAX course, by AccessLex.

A word about resentment and envy with respect to money. It may taste like a bitter pill to watch wealthier classmates or those with significant scholarships have what seems like an easy time financially, while you struggle to budget every dime. Energy spent on resentment generally does not yield productive dividends. Try to hold on, instead, to these thoughts: (1) you are you, and you are in the position you are in. Resenting someone else will not change your position. What can change your position is gaining knowledge so take a finance course for law students; (2) what you must work harder for, you may appreciate more; and (3) you don't know the full "price" someone is really paying for whatever funds that they have been given. There may be strings attached that you would never want.

CHAPTER 8

ACTIVE LEARNING

Active learning is full engagement in an affirmative quest to understand information and master skills. Passive learning is a sponge-like process of letting yourself *absorb* information. The more you interact with material, the more you will retain. Active learning also saves time. Why? When you are fully engaged you tend to "get" concepts more readily and reduce time necessary to review. One recent study found that students who listened to a bar review lecture two or more times actually did worse on the exam than those who listened once. Why? In that group, the students who repeated the lecture were likely not "on" and fully focused the first time, then had to rush through the second time, so they never absorbed the content with sufficient concentration.

Ever zone out and find yourself "reading" the same passage several times but not understanding a word? You know what I am talking about. I call this "glazing over." It's a colossal waste of time. Fight to zone in and develop active-reading skills. You will see results in comprehension and retention.

But you can't be "on," in high gear, all day every day. This is true in work and law school. You need breaks. And, you want to make the best use of both high-energy and low-energy cycles by balancing active and passive learning. When you are too tired to effectively continue high-gear work, you can sometimes still push yourself to continue studying for another few hours if you switch to a less-active task. For instance, let's say during a particular weekend you have been reading from your casebook and creating your outline. You are tired. You could take a break or call it a day and go to sleep. You could also switch to lower energy learning activity, such as listening to parts of a recorded lecture or audio book on the subject.

To help calendar both active and passive learning, you need to notice the times of day you are most and least productive and you need to determine what sorts of tasks require full engagement and what you can learn by simply letting in information. Start by completing the reflection below.

PIF: Active/Passive Learning

Categorize law school study including the following tasks as tending toward more Active or Passive: reading cases, case briefing, reading a commercial outline, creating your own outline, listening in class, taking notes in class, listening to a class recording. Then think of ways to make the passive tasks more active.

Active	Passive
_____	_____
_____	_____
_____	_____
_____	_____
_____	_____
_____	_____

Book-Ending Class

To get the most out of class, dedicate time before and after. As you complete reading assigned for each class (and, yes, do that reading before class!), check in both with the course syllabus and the casebook Table of Contents to see where you are within the subject. Look up any terms you can't readily define so that you will understand your professor more easily. And, go in with the most open and patient attitude possible. Know that if you get called on you will do your best and it will be OK. Nerves will block you from learning. Breathe deeply, and dress comfortably.

During class, listen as carefully as possible—to your professor and to your classmates. Sit up, lean forward, and listen. Zip your phone inside your backpack. For every question your professor asks, think about how you would answer, and pay close attention to how your classmate responds. Doing this is training your critical listening –a skill you will need in law practice. Think for example about how closely you will have to listen during a deposition. (If you need a "trick" to get yourself to focus, *pretend* that after every comment made in class your professor will turn to you and ask you to repeat what was said.)

ACTIVE LEARNING 55

Take notes selectively. Don't try to write down every word; this may prevent you from really *hearing* the professor and your classmates. Jot down key points to look up later. Write examples the professor mentions. Note points your professor repeats. Repeating something is a sign that it's important to that person. And often professors like to test areas they believe are important.

After class, *while the material is still fresh,* update your outline with your notes, examples, charts, lists, and tips. This will help seal in what you learned.

Create Your Own Outlines

Everyone talks about outlines. What are they? How do they help you? Outlines are logically and topically organized summaries of law school subjects. An outline sets out rules and also explains the reasoning behind relevant rules and provides examples that illustrate how particular concepts might be tested. (You can take a look at some outlines I wrote with a colleague in West's *Step-by-Step Guide to* Contracts, *Step-by-Step Guide to* Torts, and *Step-by-Step Guide to* Criminal Law. But, only look at other people's outlines for ideas; write your own.)

Some easy steps to getting started creating your own outlines:

- Start with the main headings in your syllabus and casebook table of contents. (Outlines are organized topically, not case-by-case.)
- Define all key terms and maybe include a glossary at the back of your outline.
- Write in the margins of your casebook as you read, and transfer those thoughts to your outline.
- Weave in under the relevant headings in your outline examples and concepts your professor emphasizes.
- Take particular rules and theories and make them into charts or diagrams in your outline.

- Don't worry about how long your outlines are. As the semester progresses, condense your outlines to a usable size as you get closer to exam time.
  - Open Book Finals? If you have open book finals, you may want to keep your outline long and add a very detailed table of contents so you can easily find rules during the exam. Or you may want to condense it into an easy-to-use format.
  - Closed book exams? Your outlines cannot be brought into the exam. *Only what is in your brain comes in.* So be sure you are using the outlines as learning tools, and that the most critical information gets *and stays* in your head. It can also help to work in stages, first writing as much as you need to understand, then reducing the subject to ten to thirty pages, and lastly, by the week before your final exam, summarize the content in one to three pages.

Bottom line: Outlines are only as useful as you make them. And, they are personal to you and for you—so there is no one "right" outlining technique.

Learn About Learning

Metacognition—learning how you learn and thinking about how you think—applies to all parts of law school: how you understand new concepts, how you retain knowledge, and how you apply what you know in new fact patterns on exams.

Throughout 1L, you will want to think about your learning process inside and outside of class, with others and independently. And, you want to be open to making changes and seeing what works best—based both on learning science and on your own self assessments.

For example, some people need to take notes to pay attention. For others, the opposite is true: they can't really focus and absorb concepts while writing or typing.

Some people write the relevant portion of their outline before each class and put their notes right into that outline.

ACTIVE LEARNING 57

Others take notes on blank pages then transfer points to their outline.

Some prefer handwriting notes; others prefer typing.

Don't feel peer pressured into studying or taking notes in ways that are good for others. Pay attention to learning science and to what works for you.

Bottom line, put your own spin on studying, keeping in mind that the most effective learning requires active engagement, struggle (wrestling with the material), self-testing and re-writing after studying sample answers, spaced repetition (returning to concepts at certain intervals), and putting content into context or schemas (perhaps in lists or flowcharts).

Note: what "worked" in or before college may not work in law school. Law school exams are different. You won't be asked to memorize case names or dates or other "facts." You will be asked to learn legal rules and to read critically and think logically, on the spot, as you *apply each component of those rules to brand new fact patterns.*

If your law school keeps any of your professors' old exams on file, study them. And, talk with your law librarian and ASP faculty about getting high quality practice exams. It is only by really knowing how you will be tested that you can begin to fully understand how best to prepare for those tests.

PIF: Practice Test Reflection

The following are places I can look or people in the law school I can consult to find reliable practice tests:

After I complete a practice test, I will:

After I complete a practice test, I will not:

Hint: Helpful actions after completing practice exams include: study sample answers, learn rules you don't know, and improve your organization, logical analysis, and writing. Unhelpful: judging yourself or beating yourself up. Use practice exams as *learning tools*, not predictors of how you will perform on the actual exam. Learn from every "mistake." Make improvements with every practice and study opportunity. (Yes, every study moment is a learning *opportunity!*)

CHAPTER 9

SURROUND YOURSELF WITH POSITIVE PEOPLE

"Do what you feel in your heart to be right, for you'll be criticized anyway. You'll be damned if you do and damned if you don't."

—ELEANOR ROOSEVELT—

Somewhere in the first year of law school your confidence may take a hit. It may be when you are called on in class or after a midterm or final. Or it may be a comment from a classmate or one of your professors that feels undermining.

Believing in yourself and your abilities and investing in yourself so that you have the resources to succeed, are all easier said than done, especially if you are first-gen or do not have a great support system. It is all harder still if you feel undermined. And a host of challenges can undermine:

- Imposter syndrome and/or stereotype threat based on culture, race, religion, ethnicity, gender, etc.
- A parent, grandparent, or other important person in your life who does not approve of your becoming a lawyer.
- Financial pressures that cause you to doubt the wisdom of a long-term investment in this professional career.
- Explicit comments or implicit suggestions that you are not smart enough to pass the bar exam and become a lawyer.
- People in your world who are unfamiliar with the rigors of law school and just don't get it.

You may find yourself in a relationship with someone who resents the time and energy that law school requires and either intentionally or inadvertently sabotages you. A few former students who were looking back on law school, as they prepared for the bar exam, recognized a pattern that they hadn't realized had actually started in 1L: arguments with a partner, spouse, or significant other that erupted just before *each* set of final exams. They made changes before the bar exam but wished they had seen the situation more clearly during school.

There are strategies to help build resistance against those who prey on your doubts, ways to protect yourself and claim the success you desire and deserve, and tools to dilute negative influences. As with protecting our time, we started by asking where the time goes, so too to protect against negative people, we begin by exploring who is in our world. I'll ask you to sort the people in your world into categories:

- people who are supportive and "get it"
- people who could be supportive but just need help learning how
- people who are not helpful and likely won't be any time soon
- people who are downright destructive

As you move through law school, it can be easiest to surround yourself with people who "get it." But it is helpful and important for law school success and professional success to also cultivate support from those who could and would provide it if they knew how, and to practice handling the naysayers and saboteurs—people to avoid, temporarily (such as during particularly stressful times such as finals) or permanently.

> **PIF/CCC Reflection: Supporters and Saboteurs**
>
> Complete this reflection, considering who is and is not supportive. *This is just for you.* You do not need to show anyone the lists. In fact, you may want to delete or destroy them. But, it can be useful to clarify for yourself who will and who will not be helpful during this first year of law school.

SURROUND YOURSELF WITH POSITIVE PEOPLE

Part A: List your supportive "troops." Write names and contact info for people you know "get it," people you can reach out to when you need a boost.

1. _____
2. _____
3. _____
4. _____
5. _____

Part B: List people who are supportive, but don't yet "get it."

1. _____
2. _____
3. _____
4. _____
5. _____

Part C: List potential saboteurs, individuals or classes of people such as those from a particular student organization who tend to distract you—or who are unsupportive in any other way.

1. _____
2. _____
3. _____
4. _____
5. _____

Part D: List actual saboteurs, people to avoid, or, at the very least, those whose messages need to be diluted, including individuals who have intentionally or inadvertently made destructive comments or engaged in undermining actions.

1. _____
2. _____
3. _____
4. _____
5. _____

People Who Are Supportive of You and Want to Help

Let's start with this: you want to spend some time during law school with supportive people, but your time will be limited. You will need many hours dedicated to studying and that can be all-consuming (and it may need to be just before finals). But most people are much happier with a balance throughout the semester, including allowing themselves to really enjoy time with friends and family. So, in addition to sorting supportive from unsupportive people, I strongly urge you try to be in the moment: immerse yourself in study when you are studying *and* fully enjoy time with family and friends when you take time off. Try to avoid the "I should be studying" when you are taking well-deserved breaks. It is vital to connect with the people you care about, including new friends you will make at school.

OK, now, the people who are supportive and get it are easy. You will want to spend time with them. But want about people who mean well and want to help but don't know how? You can talk with them or write them, such as with the draft language below. Of course, you will want to adapt the tone and language to make them your own.

Draft Language for Beginning Law School

Dear _____,

As you know, I started law school this fall. I know you want to support me, and I appreciate that so much. I'm reaching out to share a few thoughts on ways you can help. Thanks for listening!

First, know that my time is much more limited. I plan to study most days and weekday evenings but to take off some weekend evenings and *possibly* a half-day or full day each weekend.

I also have on my calendar and plan to join you all for [insert two events, and protect your time so that you can join for these].

But, please,

- Do not expect that I will make it to every event or dinner,
- Please do not be offended if I need to cancel or leave early to get some extra sleep,
- And, know that I will have some new commitments, studying with classmates and attending law school events.

SURROUND YOURSELF WITH POSITIVE PEOPLE   63

Second, with the steep learning curve this first semester (a huge amount of reading), in a high-stress environment, I may appear unavailable, moody, or flaky. Please don't take it personally, but,

- I may not remember everything outside of law school so feel free to (and please) remind me about things you want me to keep in mind,
- I may say "No" to some things I used to love to do, (such as weekday happy hours),
- If there are non-urgent matters you need my help with, I will ask if they can wait until after finals,
- I may not respond as promptly to texts or other messages, and I may close my social media accounts altogether during this semester,

None of this is personal. And, it's temporary! Please just know that this is a really tough period, and I cannot begin to thank you enough for your unequivocal support.

[signed]

Draft Language for the Month Before Finals

Dear _____,

Thanks for your support all semester long! Just so you know, finals are almost here. As we talked about, I will make it to Thanksgiving dinner. I'll even come early and help cook. But, I need to leave after we eat. And even though it's a holiday, the rest of that weekend I need to study. And, from Thanksgiving through mid-December **[or insert date]**, I will essentially be gone. I will return after finals, physically and mentally, and we'll plan something fun. But between now and then, please know this:

- I'm in a super high-stakes competition. Law school grades are curved; there can only be so many As, and everyone in my class is really smart. I know I will be fine if I don't get top grades, but I do want to do everything in my power to do my very best. I owe that to myself. And, I thank you for supporting me in that effort.
- I think of finals as if I am preparing to compete in a big sports event. When I am not studying, I will need to sleep, exercise, and take care of myself. I likely cannot join holiday parties or other gatherings until after finals. Feel free to tell me about

- plans, and if at the last minute I feel I've put in a productive enough study day and can get away, I will let you know.
- If there is anything you need my help with—even an important decision—please wait to ask me about it until after finals unless it truly cannot wait.
- FYI, I likely won't respond promptly or sometimes at all to messages. Apologies in advance if you think I'm ignoring you. I'm not. And I am not trying to be rude. I will check in when I can and if something is truly urgent, please label the message, "urgent." And, I will return all messages after my last exam.
- Please do not take personally any sort of moodiness or tension you sense. It has nothing to do with you. And, finals will be over soon.

I know you respect how tough this is and appreciate how much stress I'm under, and I thank you more than you will ever know for your compassion and understanding.

[signed]

As weird as this sounds, sometimes a heartfelt letter can really help. It's hard to grasp just how challenging it is, especially for family and friends who have not been to law school. They might not understand that law school doesn't give As for effort. Grades are high-stakes, on a curve, and there is a great deal of competition. The legal profession generally is *not* a holistic, feel-good world. In litigation, there are winners and losers.

Law school is certainly not all about grades. And, it is important as a law student to know that while grades are closely connected to job opportunities in your first positions (summer jobs and your first job after graduating). But do know that after that, jobs are more often obtained from references and experience than from grades.

The balance is in being aware, and controlling what you can control. You can control the process but not necessarily the outcome. My advice: focus at every turn on *learning*. If that is your constant, your anchor, you will likely be more fulfilled and less stressed. Let yourself be curious!

SURROUND YOURSELF WITH POSITIVE PEOPLE

I am not saying don't try your best. And, please work throughout law school to continuously improve grades. Improvement is tied to bar passage, and grades are considered by first employers. But remember your why (why you came to law school).

And try to see human interest in everything you are studying. The facts in the cases you are reading are real "stories." They are "reality reading," stuff that happened to real people. The law you are learning is a power tool for social change. Each right and remedy can and does fundamentally alter lives, every day. Your law degree and your work as a professional will impact the way lives are lead, businesses are run, and the way our society functions.

Your learning is vital to your future and to those you will be helping. So, give yourself the gift that is time—time to let the learning seep in, to take it in, and to understand as much as you possibly can in every subject you study in law school.

> **PIF/CCC Exercise:**
>
> Write a letter to your family explaining why law school is demanding and asking them to give you time, space, or whatever you need. *Even if you would never send such a letter, write it for yourself.* It may help clarify what you really need or want to feel supported and give you some ideas on how to move forward.
>
> Take a moment, before or after writing your letter, to think about what your graduating from law school will mean to your family and community—not to feel additional guilt or burdens but just to have some empathy for why others might feel so invested in you. You must run your own race, but it can be important to step back and see forces outside yourself that may weigh on you—positively or negatively.

If you don't like the idea of writing a letter, think of some talking points, perhaps using an example or analogy to help the person understand why law school is different. I shared this cooking reference with one student who said it helped in talking with her family.

The difference between law school and my prior education is huge. Think of it this way. We are good

> home cooks. We can easily make a delicious family dinner. Even if busy, we can throw together a tasty salad, vegetable, protein, starch, and dessert –no problem. But imagine being asked to cook a fancy meal for a special occasion, a meal that included recipes from three or four foreign countries' cuisines that you had never even tasted before –and that the dishes were being judged by people who were professional chefs from each of those countries! That's how I feel. Each of my classes is like a different foreign country. Oh, and my dishes will be rated against those prepared by others, some of whom have familiarity with these foreign cuisines. I am starting from scratch. I have to get recipes and study them; buy ingredients I've never worked with; and learn cooking terminology and techniques I'm not acquainted with. And, I will have to practice preparing each dish, repeatedly, until I get them all right.

If you or the person you are talking with is not into cooking, you might ask them to imagine you were drafted to play in a big game in a sport you never competed in and will be out there, judged alongside other players, some of whom know the sport well. Or, you might analogize to working at a brand new high-pressure tech job in a field you never studied and don't know anything about and the boss has said only some of employees will be promoted. Ask your family or friend to imagine the kind of learning curve and focus these would require, and the stress they would bring. It takes a similarly extraordinary amount of time and energy to learn the quantity of information and new testing formats required to succeed in law school.

Well-meaning family can cause additional stress with comments such as, *"What are you worried about, you've always done well."* It can be horribly stressful for first-gen students to feel as if they must succeed on behalf of the entire family or an entire community. It might help somewhere along the road to share thoughts such as:

> "I am doing my very best, but please keep your expectations in check. There is a grading curve in law school and only 10% of the class can be in the top 10%. That may not be me. I just want you to help me to focus

SURROUND YOURSELF WITH POSITIVE PEOPLE

on doing my best. I know you believe in me and support me and you may not even realize this but it feels like a lot of weight to carry everyone else's expectations, hopes, and dreams on top of all the pressure I'm putting on myself."

However you express yourself, it may help to put your thoughts into words, even for yourself.

<u>Practice Saying "No"</u>

You may have the most supportive friends and family in the world, but they may simply not *get* how intense law school is, especially just before finals. Even if you tell them clearly, they may still urge you to step away from studying. This is fine if you truly have put in productive time and want or need the time off. But know that especially in the beginning, law school seems to take more time than you think it will, especially to accomplish deep learning. The reading takes a lot longer than reading you have done before; consolidating notes and preparing outlines can be slow going, especially if you stop to look things up that you don't understand; and completing practice exams takes time because the real learning comes from both taking tests and carefully studying sample answers to see how to improve.

So, if you need to be studying or want to be studying, keep "in your pocket" some ready responses should you be faced with having to say, "No." Here are some sample dialogues just to get you thinking; please adapt them so they are suitable to interactions with people in your life.

"Can't you come to just this one birthday party?"

- Mom: "You studied all day. Now, you'll just take off tonight. I insist. It's your uncle's eightieth birthday. You can't miss that!"

- Law student, *in your head:* "But then next week is someone else's birthday, and before you know it, finals are here. Uncle is not taking my exams for me. Neither are you, Mom. I have to go in there and do it myself. Can't you just give me a break?!"

- *Actual reply*: "I would love to come. But this is a high-gear time. I have legal writing deadlines and exams are fast approaching. This weekend, I planned to meet my study group to work on our outline and take a practice exam, and I need to keep that commitment. I need that time for learning. Thank you in advance for your support. After this first semester, I'll be able to go to more family events. But I just cannot take time away from my studies now."

Note: If you want to go to the party and would enjoy a night off, if going would re-charge your batteries, go and have a good time. The balance suggested here is simply that law school and legal work often take more time than people realize. And, especially in the beginning of law school, it can help to give yourself the time you need.

HEAVY GUILT VARIATION OF "Can't you come to just this one birthday party?"

- Mom: "You have always been such a good student. Please just take off tonight. It's Uncle Joe's eightieth birthday. You know he's not doing well. It could be our last chance to see him. And, Auntie, she'll be there with all the cousins. They will all ask where you are. Besides, you study every day. I am sure you will pass all your classes with flying colors! What are you worried about? You are so smart. You've always done well at everything. You'll be fine. This is family."

- Law student, *in your head: "If Uncle Joe were dying, I would go visit him in the hospital. But he's having a party! He can't be that sick. I know what all those people will say if I fail out of law school. I cannot break my study commitments to myself. I keep that John Wooden quote on the fridge (the one I read in Prof. Berman's book). I can't go into my exams knowing that I took off for family parties and didn't work as hard as I could have!"*

> "Success is that peace of mind that comes from knowing you've done everything in your power to become the very best you're capable of becoming."
>
> —JOHN WOODEN—

- *Actual reply*: "I want to come, Mom. I love you, and I know it's important to you. Family is important to me, too, Mom. But law school is different, and the fact that I've succeeded before does not help here. I'm playing in the big leagues now. People who don't step up get left behind. You know how hard I worked to get into law school, how much you and everyone else sacrificed to see me get here. So, I will contact Uncle now and plan to visit him for a belated birthday celebration as soon as finals are over. And, thank you for understanding that I need this time now for studying.
- *You might add, if you need to:* "Imagine if you had to go see a lawyer, Mom. Let's say, God forbid, you were wrongly accused of a crime and your lawyer came to court unprepared to defend you. As you are being taken off in handcuffs, she says, 'I'm so sorry, but I had a family birthday party last night, and I just couldn't get to researching your case.' "

Family expectations differ in different cultures. Some parents expect their grown children to attend long weekly dinners and other family events, regardless of how much studying they have, even when they are no longer living at home. If this is your situation, try to find a strategy to protect as much of your time as possible.

Let's look at another family dialogue.

"I need you to take me to the doctor."

- Grandma: "I have an appointment with the doctor on Friday. I'm counting on you to take me. You know I can't take the bus anymore."

- Law student, *in your head*: *"We talked about this. I asked you to make as many non-urgent appointments as possible after finals. I know you're not going to like it, but this Friday I have a workshop at school that I cannot miss so we will have to make other arrangements for you."*

- *Actual reply*: "If this is something that can wait until after finals, please reschedule the appointment. If you must go now, let's try to think of someone else in the family who could take you." Even if this is your role in the family—you are the one who always takes your grandparent to the doctor—speak up and ask someone else to help this time. You owe this to yourself. If no one else is available, perhaps you can arrange for a taxi or rideshare. The price of making alternate arrangements may be far lower in the long run than the price of missing class or another important study commitment. Note: If you end up going to certain appointments, for yourself or a family member, bring something to read or study so you are not frustrated having to wait.

It is understandable that people in your world think law school takes less time than it does. Even lawyers sometimes forget how demanding law school is, or they re-write history and act like they hardly studied. Try to find balance but do what you need to feel comfortable. This is your journey, not anyone else's.

The happy-hour dilemma

- Friend: "Happy Hour Friday. Be there!"
- Law Student: "Dude, you know I can't. I'm studying."

SURROUND YOURSELF WITH POSITIVE PEOPLE   71

- Friend: "Chill, dude. You study all the time. You're gonna lose your friends. Pretty soon we're not going to invite you anymore. You say 'No' all the time."

- Law Student, *in your head:* *"Just because you're there drinking your weekend away doesn't mean I should. In ten years, when I'm a successful lawyer and a member of the "bar," you may still be sitting here drinking at this bar. Yeah, but who am I kidding? I so wish I could go! Maybe just this one night? I could take off just tonight? But I shouldn't. I really have to focus and take care of myself."*

- *Actual reply:* "Keep inviting me. I'll try to stop by Friday if I can, and as soon as the semester ends, I am all over it. [Pause.] Thanks for supporting me! You might need a close friend who's a lawyer someday—ha! Kidding, Dude! But seriously, I'll be back after finals."

Don't be embarrassed about your priorities. Real friends will remember how hard you worked, support your successes, and refer clients to you when you are licensed.

Read the last sample dialogue below, then try to write your own hypothetical conversation with someone who asks something of you that you want to say, 'No" to.

The unhelpful study buddy

- Friend: "Want to come study with me at the library?"

- Law Student: "Nah, I'm gonna study alone today."

- Friend: "Come on. A bunch of us are going. We'll all help each other. Then we'll go out for some beers after."

- Law student, *in your head:* *"Your idea of studying is 80 percent chitchat and 20 percent study. Working with you is not productive for me, and I know it. I end up helping you, but all you really do is distract me."*

- *Actual reply*: "Thanks for asking. Another time. If I get enough done today, though, I'll see where you guys are and maybe meet up. Otherwise, see you in class tomorrow."

Sometimes you want to study with friends, and that's great—if it's productive. Only you know what works for you. The key is not to say, "Yes," if you know if would be best to work on your own, or sleep.

Commitments you make to yourself are as important as those you make to others. Would you flake if you were going to an appointment with a doctor or specialist you had waited months to see? No, of course not. You wouldn't even think of canceling on a client, would you? Your studies must be as important as commitments you make to others. Don't be a "no-show" on yourself.

If you live with family or roommates, you may want to post your study schedule so they don't distract you during your "study hours."

Take Breaks

Remember, breaks are helpful. After a good break, we return to work feeling more productive. But it is up to you to know yourself and give yourself what you need when you need it, be it concentrated study time or a study break that replenishes the well and boosts your energy. Just as you protect your study time, protect time for breaks as well.

PIF Reflection: Productive Ways to Say No

How often do you say, "Yes," when you want to say "No"? Write a sample dialogue involving a situation where you are asked to do something that is not productive for you. Note the person's request, what you think when you hear it, and what you might actually say by way of response.

_____
_____
_____

Saboteurs

We discussed people who mean well but don't know how to be supportive. There will be others who are not supportive at all, some intentionally and others inadvertently. To better deal with people who may try to sabotage you, it can be helpful to think about dividing them into categories:

- Family, classmates and maybe even professors whom you can't eliminate from your world so you must deal with,
- Acquaintances or strangers who you can easily distance from, and
- Possibly some friends or even a partner you ultimately decide to "let go."

One particularly hard situation is a partner, parent, or other relative who really didn't want you to go to law school in the first place. Even if you're financing it yourself, and not asking for a dime, people may disapprove of your career choice. When comments or disapproval come from these people, it hurts. For self-preservation, you must believe that your legal education and pursuit of a license to practice law are important, worthy goals. When you are studying, especially for finals, you must get away (literally or figuratively) from the negativity.

Another tough situation involves unsupportive classmates. I am sorry to say this, but forced curves and class rankings too often create "winners" and "losers" in law school. And some law students are full of themselves and so self-absorbed that they make comments they don't even realize are insulting. Others try intentionally to intimidate. They may casually claim that they study 15 hours a day and only "need" 4 hours of sleep. Some claim they don't study at all.

Don't listen to any of it. They're probably not telling the truth. It's tough to study so much in any meaningful way without sleeping, and it's impossible to do well in law school without studying at all. And, even if that is what someone else does or doesn't do, you must stay focused on your own work and self-care, and stick to your own schedule.

Use positive peer pressure *only if* it helps motivate you. Negative peer pressure is usually a waste of time and something you are best off ignoring. This is *your* law school success journey.

Try to get as far away as possible from negative people, in law school and in life. If you must deal with negative people, try to be "Teflon." Don't let their comments stick.

Yet another challenge is a negative encounter with a professor. If this is during class, you might first try to shrug it off. There is a good chance the professor doesn't really think less of you and was deliberately trying to prepare you for tough judges and opposing counsel. If it's still bothering you, though, you might try talking with that professor during office hours. You might have an altogether different impression after meeting one-on-one. And, be sure to talk with other professors with whom you do feel comfortable and respected.

Don't let the judgment or perceived judgment of one person sink in or dictate how you view yourself. You control what you let bother you. Work hard to keep the negatives out.

When anyone is rude to you, consider the possibility that they may just be having a bad day and taking it out on you. They perhaps don't think they are being rude or they don't even hear the condescension or incivility in their voices. You have the choice to ask yourself, "Does this really matter?" "Does this deserve my energy (and precious time!) getting irritated or hurt or offended?"

I had a rotten encounter at an airport during the writing of this book—incredible and needless display of disrespect from an airplane employee. I had to check my anger along with my bags. I tried the same strategy I was writing to you about. I asked myself, "Will this matter in a few hours, days, or weeks?" I could feel my shoulders relax, my heartrate return to normal, as I spoke softly to myself, 'This guy doesn't even know me. Let it go.'

Realize too that law is not a profession that specializes in nurturing. You will find many who are arrogant and treat you as "less than." It does not mean you are. Know who you are and why you are in law school. Work harder in law school (and to pass the bar exam after you graduate) and as a lifelong professional than you have ever worked on anything *because you*

SURROUND YOURSELF WITH POSITIVE PEOPLE

want to be your best. Let not the ignorance of any one person hinder your pursuit of your own success. And try not to let stereotypes that you might hold about yourself, or that others might believe about you, get in the way.

"We gain strength, and courage, and confidence by each experience in which we really stop to look fear in the face . . . we must do that which we think we cannot."

—ELEANOR ROOSEVELT—

Acquaintances or complete strangers can also be unhelpful, for example random people who are just dying to tell you bar exam horror stories or annoying lawyer jokes. Not helpful. And there will be those who say dumb things like, "You seem so argumentative; you'll definitely be #1 in your class." Such comments are just "noise"—their noise, not yours. You don't have to listen. Have a ready response or be prepared to change the subject or walk away so you don't feel cornered into talking about law school with people who are not supportive.

Remember, it really is hard to deal with people seeking to undermine you. Stay strong. Remember *who you are*. If you were not the kind of person who thrived when challenged, it's doubtful that you would have applied to law school in the first place.

Seek out regular boosts and pep talks from people you feel support you and really understand what you are going through.

Stay away as much as possible from people who are destructive.

If you are surrounded by all positive people, great! Be thankful. But too many people *do* think and talk in ways that can deeply hurt someone trying to succeed in law school. If people in your family or community do not support your becoming a lawyer, do not "buy in" to their negativity. You have every right to be proud of earning a law degree and seeking to obtain a law license. There are still gender stereotypes that women lawyers are aggressive, and there are especially hateful tropes about women of color. Don't let them in.

Law school will help you write and speak more persuasively and think more critically. Graduating and passing the bar provide credible and powerful evidence that you can perform effectively under extreme pressure. These skills will help you manage, lead, and be responsible for the lives and livelihoods of others, if you so choose. That is a good thing. You know that, and it may not be worth the effort to try to change the minds of negative folks in your life, at least not right now. Finish 1L (and maybe all of law school and the bar exam), with the help of supportive people, and *then* try to bring the others around.

Finally, let in the possibility that you might just have to let some people go. . . .

PIF Reflection: Self-Sabotage

In this chapter we looked at how others support or sabotage you. Take a moment and think about how you do the same.

1. Two ways I support myself are:

    a. _____

    b. _____

2. Two ways I sabotage myself are:

    a. _____

    b. _____

Now, list several steps you can take to maximize the ways you can boost yourself up and minimize the ways you drag myself down:

_____

_____

_____

_____

_____

_____

SURROUND YOURSELF WITH POSITIVE PEOPLE

Finally, what is some language (in your own words) that you can use to get out of conversations with potential or actual saboteurs?

CHAPTER 10

TURN PANIC INTO POWER, ANXIETY INTO ADRENALINE

As the semester progresses, you may find your worries getting in the way. There are many good reasons to feel anxious during law school. One is that there is just a lot of work to do, and it may feel like too much. Another is that people may not be supportive. And, a third is that you may just be exhausted which makes coping even harder.

It sometimes helps to try to put your nerves in a box—and let them out at a designated weekly "worry time." Note, I am not saying, "Just don't worry." I am saying try to manage your nerves so they don't derail you. And, I'll also repeat many times, especially if you have substance use issues or feel you want to harm yourself, seek treatment from a mental health professional. Ask your Dean of Students for a referral if you don't know where to get help.

"Courage is a special kind of knowledge: the knowledge of how to fear what ought to be feared and how not to fear what ought not to be feared."

—DAVID BEN-GURION—

What to do when you're blocked by law school nerves? Let's consider some different strategies for different times you feel yourself getting nervous. See if any of these help. Before we get to these: please seek help if you need or want it from a professional, a therapist or counselor in your law school or community (or from a local Lawyer's Assistance Program.) And again, please ask your Dean of Students if you need a referral.

If anxiety prevents forward movement while studying, the immediate mission is to get the intellectual flow going again.

Take three deep breaths and try reading aloud. Sometimes just that switch helps.

It may also help to stop the reading or briefing and just rewrite or copy some examples from class notes into your outline. This can be calming because it lets your mind take a break from having to think, and just the physical act of handwriting or typing sometimes helps bolster understanding. As you write or type, tell yourself, "I get this. This example makes sense, especially as I am slowly re-writing it." Smile, and force yourself to keep taking deep breaths in and out. Stay in as positive a frame of mind as possible.

If the nerves hit as you are approaching final exams, visualize yourself in the exam room. Picture yourself thinking and your words flowing. Imagine doing this in a room full of palpable stress (perhaps picturing the place you took the LSAT or SAT). Recall the nervous energy you had then and how you prevailed in spite of it. Maybe part of you thrived on the challenge! Envision yourself now and on your upcoming exams reading the questions and writing your answers, feeling calm, confident, and in control (three C's you want to keep close).

These steps may help any time nerves hit, even during exams:

- Breathe deeply and slowly—counting to three in and three out. Slow, steady, deep breaths will often release the nerves and "paralysis" that comes from them. We tend to tense up when we are nervous, and often forget to breathe properly. You will read more clearly *and think more clearly* when the oxygen is flowing freely.
- Stand up, stretch your arms, and sit back down.
- Talk to yourself, calmly and positively. Tell yourself that you *can* do this. Say it aloud several times each day. Banish from your mind any past test-taking experiences that were not positive. Replace them with empowering images of you conquering challenges. Rid your speech (and mind) of all that is not positive and strong.

It can help to talk with a supportive friend, professor, or counselor. But do remember that you will be alone during final exams, so work to also find ways to calm yourself if possible. One former student said she got through anxiety attacks during exams by telling herself that it was "just another practice test." When she felt the pressure mount, she whispered to herself, over and over like a mantra, *"This is just another practice test. You've got this. It's OK. You know what to do. Just keep reading and thinking. It's a puzzle; it all fits together. Breathe. It's just another practice test, it's just another practice test."* It helped!

There are many things you can do to de-stress outside of class or outside of an exam room, such as drink a cup of tea, take a walk, go to a yoga class, meditate, take a hot bath, or talk with someone who loves and supports you. But it is important to also develop some effective calming habits that you can employ if you find yourself panicking *during exams.*

And, by far *the most effective tool to combat law school nerves is adequate preparation.* The better your training, the more prepared you are, the less your nerves will hinder you. If you do feel nervous on midterms and finals, which is totally normal no matter how hard you studied, you will be much more able to turn the nervousness into adrenaline so it serves, rather than defeats.

Don't just ignore the nerves and tell yourself you'll do fine on exams because you did well in college. Law school is different. Learn about what is tested on law school exams and in what format, and practice. Turn **panic** into **power** not **paralysis**.

If people tell you just "don't be nervous" or suggest that it is stupid or weird to be nervous, they are either ignorant and need a "reality check," or just plain full of garbage. It is *normal* to be nervous. If you are not at least a little nervous, you likely do not appreciate the seriousness of what you are doing. You might find it helpful and consoling when others share that they too are nervous. It may make you feel less alone. But nerves are sometimes contagious and cause you to stress out further. If that's the case for you, don't talk about anxiety with classmates. Talk instead with a school counselor or your ASP faculty. You must protect yourself as you prepare for success.

Similarly, sometimes you can talk yourself out of panic, but other times even thinking about it just gets you worked up further. If that sort of nervousness hits, try to switch gears, take a break, or take a nap/sleep. Figure out now if you are someone who can let stress go when you air it, or someone who obsesses further and gets more stressed out.

> **PIF Reflection: Dealing with Anxiety**
>
> List three things that you have done in the past to successfully combat or manage nerves or anxiety:
>
> 1.
>
> 2.
>
> 3.
>
> List one new thing you might try if you panic while studying and two possible tools to calm yourself if you feel anxiety during exams:
>
> 1.
>
> 2.
>
> 3.

Again, though we are talking about strategies that one can sometimes employ independently, it may be necessary and it may be best to seek out and talk with a professional. If you are not sure, try meeting with your Dean of Students.

Reframing

One powerful way to self-talk through certain anxieties is to reframe negative or stressful thoughts. Note: If you have a hard time reframing thoughts for yourself, just imagine how you might rephrase for a friend. Consider the following examples:

- *Thought*: I can't believe the professor called on me on the one day I wasn't prepared. I feel like such an idiot. And, I'm sure everyone in the class thinks I am stupid.
- *Rephrase*: I am pretty darn proud of myself that I've been prepared for class on most every day, and I could not have known I'd be called on then. And, even unprepared, I was polite and responded as best I could. No one thinks less of

TURN PANIC INTO POWER, ANXIETY INTO ADRENALINE

me. And, what really matters is that I am doing the best I can and moving forward.

Your Turn

- *Thought*: I know I'm not as smart as my classmates. What if I can't make it in law school?
- **Rephrase:** _____
- *Thought*: This case briefing is ridiculous. My "briefs" are still longer than the cases! I'll never learn to do this. I must just use canned briefs and stop trying.
- **Rephrase:** _____
- *Thought*: There is too much reading. I can't do it. I give up.
- **Rephrase:** _____
- *Thought*: I still don't understand what is going on here. People are using all kinds of words that just don't make sense to me. Maybe I don't belong.
- **Rephrase:** _____

Your rephrasing may sound different and that is fine, but here below are just some possibilities of how you might reframe and rephrase the previous examples:

- *Old Thought*: I know I'm not as smart as my classmates. What if I can't make it in law school?
- **Rephrase:** OK, wait, I *earned* my spot in this class just as everyone else here did. It is normal that it's hard. I will continue to do my best, one day at a time. And, I'll get help if I need it. I can always make appointments with my professors, ASP faculty, or the Dean of Students.
- *Old Thought*: This case briefing is ridiculous. My "briefs" are still longer than the cases! I'll never learn to do this. I must just use canned briefs and stop trying.
- **Rephrase:** Case briefing is not supposed to be easy, especially at first. I must keep at it. I will get the hang of it.
- *Old Thought*: There is too much reading. I can't do it. I give up.

- ***Rephrase:*** My critical reading muscles will get a work out here, that's for sure. I will gradually increase the time I spend reading each day so that I work up to being able to focus for longer and longer stretches. I will try to complete the readings at the same time every day, and read when I've rested and focused—not when multi-tasking. I will work to find a study spot where I can concentrate. I will see where cases fit in to the syllabus and the casebook table of contents before I read so I have context for what I am reading.
- *Thought*: I still don't understand what is going on here. People are using all kinds of words that just don't make sense to me. Maybe I don't belong.
- ***Rephrase:*** Law school is like being in a foreign country so of course I don't understand stuff. This *is* a whole new language. I know it will take time, but I will start looking up words and phrases I don't get. Eventually I will speak and write this language fluently. It may not feel like I fit in today, especially not compared to people whose parents are lawyers. But they are on their journey and I am on mine. I will work on making connections, figure out the system, and before I know it, the years will zip by and I'll be a lawyer.

It can be helpful to practice reframing every time you catch yourself in a panicked or negative thought spiral—possibly by just saying the word: "Rephrase."

I'll pause here to reiterate a caveat noted throughout this book: do not hesitate to consult a professional, a therapist, counselor, or your local LAP (Lawyers Assistance Program—free and confidential)—if you want or need help and particularly if you are using substances to cope or engaging in or want to engage in self harm.

Is your study space stressful?

Some people just cannot focus at a cluttered desk, but for others it's seriously anxiety producing. Certain people love the law library; others just enter the library and feel panicked.

Your goal is to find and/or create a study space that helps your brain to flow, a place where you can remain steadily in a calm and focused state of mind.

> **PIF Reflection: Location, Location, Location**
>
> 1. What are your first thoughts when you sit in your study space?
>
> 2. Do your surroundings distract you?
>
> 3. Does the place you study help you focus? Why or why not?

Burnout

Some people *start* law school burned out. Others are just really dragging by the semester's midpoint. If you are suffering from burnout, it's important to assess what you need to recharge your batteries. Do you need a half day, full day, or entire weekend off? Would fresh air and a change of scenery clear your mind?

Sometimes you must take a good chunk of time completely off. Other times you can find great boosts of energy from small changes, such as giving yourself consistent rewards *each day* just for doing your best, a slightly bigger one each week, a major reward each month, and great one after finals are over.

What makes you smile, feel happy, or comforted? What works for you? Is it movies or TV? Gourmet food or wine? Give yourself some special treat at the end of a hard day's learning—chocolate, ice cream, sautéed mushrooms in truffle oil? (Well, I said whatever works for you!) Once a week or month, go out to a special restaurant or cook, or have someone else cook, a special meal at home. At the end of the semester, plan and cook an elaborate dinner party for someone or some people who supported you during the semester.

If it's music, try a 15-minute "dance party" to your favorite tunes every afternoon. Once a week or month, go listen to live music somewhere. Buy tickets in advance for a great concert at the end of the semester. Whenever you feel overwhelmed, overloaded, tired, fearful, or discouraged, try playing or singing music that makes your spirit sing. Even during exams, if you find yourself slowing down or in a moment of panic, humming an uplifting tune in your head may be just the secret weapon to pull you through. Create law school playlists—mellow ones to wind down with and upbeat ones to motivate with!

> What's on your playlist?
> - What songs wake you up and motivate you to study?
> - What songs help you relax and unwind after studying?

Beware of slipping into negative self-talk and self-defeating thoughts. Your thoughts become your beliefs, so your own words can become your saboteurs. Yes, it will be hard to maintain a consistently positive attitude. You will get tired and frustrated. There will be people and classes you do not like (or like less than others). But you have more control than you may realize over how much you let the negativity in.

Assume you are midway through 1L. Which of the following best describes your feelings? Choose one of the following:

A. I'm dying here—trying to fit in and hating it!

B. I am in the worst section. My profs make things more confusing not less so.

C. I'll never be able to do all the work they expect of me.

D. I'm training to become a lawyer—slowly and steadily. It's really hard and it's supposed to be that way. It's not personal. I can view every challenge as something that will make me stronger. I have the choice as to how I look at things. I will continue to figure out where I need help and seek it out. I'll take it one day at a time, and I will be fine. I will remind myself, especially on tough days, that this is a long-term investment.

Try to make D your answer. You may use different words, but you get the point.

You might genuinely fear that doing well in law school is simply too ambitious of a goal. It's entirely normal to feel fear.

TURN PANIC INTO POWER, ANXIETY INTO ADRENALINE

The key is not to let it stop you. Do not be afraid of fear. Use it. Turn anxiety into adrenaline, *panic* into *power* not *paralysis*.

Let fear make you more motivated—perhaps in a commitment to study more or in a more focused manner. Or use fear to create energy that can combat test anxiety. Lean into it. When you feel the fear, tell yourself it's a good thing, it's your ally, and let it pump you up. Try meditation, breathing exercises, and mantras you can repeat to yourself to help restore a state of calm so you can continue studying and moving forward.

As we have said repeatedly, if your levels of anxiety are very high, if you cannot manage them or are using substances to cope, or if you feel that you may harm yourself, get professional help. As a law student, you have resources. You have support.

And, you may be surprised how much it can help to just talk with someone who *gets* it—especially if you are the first in your family to go to law school. Sometimes all you need is one person to believe in you to help you believe in yourself. And do not be too quick to rule out people with different challenges; they may empathize with your struggles and provide just the support you need.

If you experience particular doubts or anxiety because you are part of a historically underrepresented population, know that you are not alone and find someone to talk with. If you cannot find someone in your law school, reach out to a recent alum or someone in the community. And, remember that your legal education can be a power tool to help fight prejudice, dismantle stereotypes, and make the world a better place so that others don't have to face the same challenges you do.

CCC/PIF Reflection:

- What are your greatest challenges in law school?

  _____

- What do you think are the challenges facing your classmates?

  _____

- Describe challenges others face that are not an issue for you:

- Describe challenges you face that you don't believe others have to deal with:

- How will dealing with today's challenges inform how you view the challenges your future clients will face?

- Who can you talk with who will get it and/or be supportive?

Learn from Mistakes

Law students are often over cautious; they fear making mistakes. This may begin by being humiliated in class or in a study group. Some professors view law school precisely as the place where law students must learn to toughen up so they will not fall apart when facing a hostile judge or contentious opposing counsel. Sometimes this "training" strengthens students, but sometimes it makes them all the more fearful.

Caution may indeed be the hallmark of a good lawyer; an ounce of prevention can sometimes save your client millions of dollars. But some of the best learning comes from making mistakes, and you will be well served if you can develop a thick skin during law school.

Know that *some mistakes are good*, especially when they are in "low stakes, high value" settings such as practice tests or answering something wrong in class. (Why do I say class is low stakes? Because most law schools grade anonymously.)

PIF Reflection:

- Describe a past mistake and what you learned from it.

TURN PANIC INTO POWER, ANXIETY INTO ADRENALINE

- Do you fear making mistakes, and if so why?

- Are there lower stakes mistakes that you can make without negative consequences? Name one.

The wonderful thing about even your small success stories, your own daily victories, is that they become part of a virtuous cycle; they help you believe that you can succeed again and again in the future.

I keep a picture on my desktop of a woman punching her fist through a brick wall, shattering the wall, as a reminder of the inner force it takes to break through barriers. What sort of picture might help you? Maybe it's a photo of a person who was the first to achieve a particular goal you admire. Or maybe it's a video clip from a powerful courtroom scene.

PIF Reflection: Feeling Your Power

Take a moment and describe an image that makes you feel strong.

If you feel weaker or less than from certain aspects of law school, can you think of an approach or response that would empower you? (For example, if "cold calling" feels intimidating, would it help to think of it as a non-graded "game" or a "low stakes" "dress rehearsal" for dealing with a nasty opposing counsel?)

Think of a time in your past when you have felt powerful. What were you wearing, saying, doing, thinking?

Imagine yourself working as an attorney. How will you feel your power as a professional?

Chapter 11

What Is IRAC?

Somewhere in 1L, maybe even at Orientation, you will hear about "IRAC," an acronym that stands for Issue, Rule, Analysis (or Application, or Argument), Conclusion. You will see below, that I prefer the word "Proof" to "Analysis" so I'll suggest IRPC instead of IRAC, but more on that below. For now, what is IRAC? IRAC is a tool—a template or system—to guide exam writing in a logical manner, using facts to prove or disprove elements of rules of law.

Some people will tell you that you must use IRAC to write law exams. Others will say not to use IRAC, particularly not in any kind of wooden way. What that may mean here is that you should not use the terms themselves, "issue," "rule," or "analysis," as headings. But, it is almost always helpful to employ strategies to logically resolve questions about liability or guilt in new fact patterns. And that's really all IRAC really is—a logical strategy or template to reason through new fact patterns.

We will look at the parts of IRAC here so that you know what they are and so that you understand the logic behind them. You can then practice with resources at your law school, so that you are as prepared as possible for exams.

Remember, what your professor says is most important and overrides anything anyone else says. Listen to the people that will be grading your exams.

And, take practice exams throughout the semester. Do not "Do the Ostrich" and tell yourself that because you took exams in college you know how to write law school exams. *Law school exams are different.* Seize any opportunities you might have to complete practice exams and study sample answers to improve—*especially if your professors have released exams.*

Again, listen carefully for anything your professors say about how they will test and what their exams will and won't cover.

Ask faculty in your law school's academic support program and/or law librarians for resources to find practice exams.

And check out some of the many helpful books and supplements about how to write successful law school exams. Many of these resources are free to you as part of a law school subscription. Talk with your law librarians.)

> **In second semester of 1L?**
>
> If you are in your second semester, take a hard look at your exams from first semester and find any ways you can to improve going forward. Meet with each of your professors and ask them how your exam answers could have been improved. Listen and take notes. Don't ask for a grade change unless there's been a computational error, and don't be defensive. Just be curious, listen, and take in any advice on how to improve.

With exams as with other parts of life, the road to success is yours, but only if you drive. If you are only a passive passenger, you may get lucky but you may not. Take control of the controllables, including final exams. They will be here before you know it. You can walk in knowing you have done everything in your power to achieve success, or knowing you could have done more. Your choice.

Back to IRAC. As we said, IRAC stands for Issue, Rule, Analysis (or Application or Argument).

Issue

An "issue" is a question to be resolved. There are typically main issues and sub-issues in law school exams. In a criminal law question, for example, a main issue might be whether or not the defendant is guilty of any crimes and if so why. Sub-issues might focus on whether or not facts sufficiently prove each element of each relevant offense and of any applicable defense theories.

We will look more at issue spotting and practice with it. But a most important point to understand is that the more thorough your knowledge of the rules of law, the more readily you will see "issues." When you know the elements of particular rules really

WHAT IS IRAC? 93

well, including how they have been interpreted by courts, the words that "trigger" discussions of related issues just pop right out as you read new fact patterns. The keys are thus to learn the law and to practice analyzing past exams and sample answers.

Rule

The "rules" are often the most straightforward part of the IRAC. I'm not saying rules are easy to learn, or memorize if you have closed book exams. Rules are not just what the words state but how they have been interpreted. For example, burglary used to be restricted to dwellings and now extends to most any protected structure; it used to only be a crime at nighttime but now can be committed at any time. You learn rule interpretations through law school reading and studying.

I am saying that when you have learned rules (and you know which rule applies and where), you will simply state those rules word for word on your exam. You will not earn points for phrasing rules in any fancy or original way.

Note: Use particular terminology or phrasings that your professor suggests.

Analysis

"Analysis" is typically the trickiest part of IRAC—and the part which is given the most credit. On well-written law school exams, the analysis portion is deep and thoughtful, with analogies to and distinctions from caselaw studied during the semester, policy concerns, and subtleties or relevant changes within or interpretations of the law itself. It may be helpful to reference majority and minority positions in evolving areas of law or compare older case law to more modern trends you have studied.

But, before adding bells and whistles, it can help to understand the basic logic of this part of exam writing. In your "analysis," you are writing how the facts from the exam fact pattern *prove* or *disprove* each element (component part) of each applicable legal rule. For this reason, I tend to call the "analysis" portion of IRAC "proof." More on proof below.

Conclusion

Following the analysis and flowing from the analysis is the conclusion, the logical resolution of the issue(s) being analyzed. Note: each sub-issue may need a mini-conclusion and each main issue or larger dispute will need a global conclusion that answers the main question(s) asked.

> **CRAC or CRIAC: Start with conclusions?**
>
> Some professors prefer writing in a CRAC (conclusion, rule, analysis, conclusion) or CRIAC (conclusion, rule, issue, analysis, conclusion) format rather than IRAC. This does not change the basic logic. If you are advised to write in CRAC style and you are not sure who will prevail until you finish writing, write in IRAC style and then cut and paste your conclusion at the top of your discussion.

> **Issue-Spotting Exercise**
>
> Consider the sentence: *"The defendant entered the Miller office building at dusk through an unlocked door to get the umbrella that he had left, then saw the diamond ring, took it, and walked out into the rain."* If the question asked about the defendant's possible guilt for burglary, what potential sub-issues do each of the following words or phrases trigger?
>
> "office building at dusk"
>
> _____
> _____
> _____
>
> "through an unlocked door"
>
> _____
> _____
> _____
>
> "that he had left"
>
> _____
> _____
> _____

WHAT IS IRAC? 95

"then"

To identify legal issues, you must know the applicable rule(s). Here: Common law burglary is defined as the breaking and entering of the dwelling house of another in the nighttime with intent to commit a felony therein. **(Note: if you did not know the rule, you could not effectively issue spot.)** With the rule in mind, though, you might ask questions such as:

1. Does the "office building" satisfy the "dwelling house" element of burglary? (Here, you likely reminded yourself that modern jurisdictions have extended this element to include any "protected structure.")

2. And, do the words "at dusk" satisfy the "in the nighttime" element? (This element too has been eliminated under modern law.)

3. Does entering through an unlocked door satisfy the "breaking" element?

4. Is the defendant's going inside to get the umbrella "that he had left" sufficient to prove he had the requisite mens rea, or "intent to commit a felony therein"? He may not have had any criminal intent if he walked in to retrieve his own property.

5. Does the word "then" raise a potential issue? It may be relevant to the question of when the possibly felonious intent was formed, timing being critical to culpability.

A Deeper Dive into Analysis

The issue spotting and analysis portions of an exam answer, particularly the analysis, are typically given much more weight than rule recitation or conclusion sections. The assumption is that everyone can learn the rules, but differences are often reflected in how effectively students are able to spot and analyze issues. Professors often lament weak analysis calling it, "conclusory." What this usually means is that there is insufficient factual support for a statement—or that the answer does not articulate sufficient reasoning and proceeds to a conclusion without a logical foundation. Your goal will be to try to use all the facts in the fact pattern.

Some students find the "analysis" portion of law school exams to be particularly confusing because the term itself can be misleading. Students hear the word "analysis," and think of complex wrinkles in the weeds of legal theories and reasoning; they picture lengthy, Socratic questioning and endless "what ifs." Classroom exchanges are designed to promote detailed understanding of case law, and to test the boundaries of various rules. Class is often far more complicated than the logic of an exam structure.

Other students hear the word "analysis" and think of a layered literary analysis from a college English class, reflecting perhaps on the meaning, style, and moral value of a novel or poem. Writing literary or political analyses are not the same as writing the analysis portion of a law school essay exam.

IRAC as "IRPC"

As noted above, it may help in the context of a law school essay exam to think of the word *"Proof"* as a synonym for "Analysis." A useful mental picture, at least as a starting point, requires a flashback to middle school geometry and the logic contained in a basic proof. (For those who hated math, sorry!)

Let's start with this oversimplified simple triangle example:

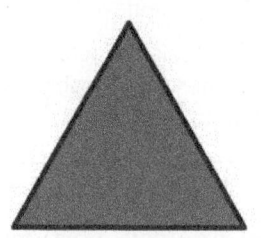

What sort of figure is this image? **[ISSUE]**

Three-sided figures with sides coming together at three corners are generally known as *triangles*. An equilateral triangle is a three-sided figure in which all three sides are equal in length and all three corners have the same degree angle. **[RULE]**

Here, side A measures x inches, side B measures x inches, and side C measures x inches. The three sides meet at three corners, each with an angle measuring y degrees. **[PROOF (or analysis)]**

WHAT IS IRAC? 97

Therefore, the figure is an equilateral triangle. **[CONCLUSION]**

Now, let's consider another example, this one using an everyday driving scenario in which you will see the same sort of logic but in a situation that more closely resembles a law-type fact pattern. Note here that we will also add a policy consideration to our logical writing. Policy concerns are critical to some professors while not as much to others. As long as you have written about all the discussable legal issues, correctly using the basic components of an IRPC—*and you finish answering the entire question*—adding policy considerations may indicate a further mastery of the application of the rule of law that a professor may appreciate.

> The defendant and his passenger, Witness X, both testified that the defendant's car was in the left-turn lane, the green arrow was blinking, and it was 3:00 p.m. when the turn was made. Did the defendant's turn from Elm Street onto Main Street on December 1 violate traffic regulations?

Now let's say you learned that left turns are permitted from the left-turn lane at the intersection of Elm and Main when the green left-turn arrow is blinking at times other than 4:00pm to 7:00pm on weekdays. (From 4:00pm to 7:00pm on weekdays, such turns are not permitted even if the arrow is green.) Now, using an "IRPC" format, how would we logically deconstruct the legality of the turn in question?

Did the defendant's 3:00pm left turn at Elm and Main violate traffic laws with respect to turning? **[ISSUE]**

Left turns are permitted at the intersection of Elm and Main from the left-turn lane when the green left-turn arrow is blinking and at times other than between 4:00pm and 7:00pm on weekdays. **[RULE]**

Here, the defendant was in the left-turn lane (the proper location to make a left turn). He saw the turn arrow blinking (the signal that it was safe to make his turn). The defendant made the turn in question at 3:00pm (an appropriate time for this type of turn). It is unclear what day of the week it was but since the turn was 3:00pm, that would not matter as turns are only restricted between 4:00pm and 7:00pm. **[PROOF or analysis]**

Note: policy would dictate that even if the defendant had followed the technical requirements for turning, he must have also confirmed that it was generally safe to make the turn, i.e. that there were no other obstacles, emergency vehicles, or unanticipated conditions that would make the turn unsafe. Assuming the defendant did confirm such general safety concerns, there is no indication that the turn was unlawful. **[POLICY** (optional)**]**

Therefore, the defendant's turn from Elm onto Main appears to have been lawful. **[CONCLUSION]**

This is straightforward, right? It makes sense. It is not mysterious or intriguing. It is not eloquent or fancily worded. It is simple and direct, logical and organized.

One of my law school professors once explained exam writing something like this: "Many of you came to law school from lofty colleges where you theorized and studied literature and history and the like. You read poetry and wrote beautiful essays. You sought to include metaphors and alliteration, so that your words would flow. You want to continue that sort of writing now, in law school. Your minds are creative. You *want* to think, 'Well, I'll start by discussing A; but then let me foreshadow Z; then I'll get back to B; and maybe then toss in a bit of H and J to make things more vibrant.' " He then pounded the podium and hollered, "No!" in such a booming voice that everyone in the class jumped. "Cut that out right now! From here on, instead of flowery prose, it's A + B + C = D. Period."

Show Your Work

Law students who are trained as professionals in other fields or who have worked in law offices and are used to clients seeking quick answers often find it challenging to slow down and write each step of their thinking. My law students who are medical doctors going back to law school frequently say, "The patient doesn't want a long story. She just wants the diagnosis and treatment. Basically, she would be thrilled if I didn't say anything other than, 'Take this. It will make you feel better.' " Clients who are paying for services also often want instant answers. Law professors are more like good math teachers; they want to "see your work," your ability to reason logically, step by step.

Let's try another scenario, this time involving a potential breach of contract.

QUESTION

The plaintiff, Andrea, claims that after a series of negotiations, she asked the Defendant, Daniel, and Daniel orally agreed on September 22 to buy Andrea's stamp collection for $15,000. Daniel claims that Andrea asked if Daniel wanted to buy her stamp collection, that Daniel said he would buy her stamp collection for that price but only if Andrea also included her coin collection, and that Andrea said she would think about it and get back to Daniel. Do Andrea and Daniel have a binding contract? Discuss.

Write your own answer to this question:

Next, after writing your own answer, read the sample answer below, and, in each bracket, note whether the text prior to that bracket represents an issue, rule, analysis (proof) or conclusion.

Sample Answer

<u>Do Daniel and Andrea Have a Valid Contract?</u> [_____]

A contract may be defined as a promise or set of promises for breach of which the law gives a remedy, or the performance of which the law in some way recognizes a duty. To find a valid contract exists there must be mutual assent (as evidenced by a valid offer and a valid acceptance) supported by valid consideration. Further there can be no defenses to the formation of a valid contract that would negate the validity of the contract in question.

<u>Offer?</u> [_____]

Did Andrea offer to sell the stamp collection? [_____] An offer is a promise to do or refrain from doing some specified thing in the future conditioned on the other party's acceptance. To be a valid offer, the offeror must demonstrate a commitment with sufficiently definite terms communicated to an identified offeree. [_____] It would appear that Andrea did make a valid offer to sell the stamp collection. Both parties concur that she asked and there is a demonstration of a commitment in Andrea's asking. She asked Daniel (an identifiable offeree) if he wanted to buy a particular item (a specific stamp collection) for a definite price ($15,000) thus with sufficiently definite terms.

She has communicated definite terms. She is not simply inquiring or thinking about possibly offering later. [_____] Therefore, it appears that Andrea made a valid offer.[_____]

<u>Acceptance?</u> [_____]

Has Daniel accepted Andrea's offer? [_____] An acceptance is a voluntary act of the offeree whereby the offeree exercises the power conferred by the offeror and thereby creates the set of legal relations called a contract. [_____] Here, Daniel contends that he said he would only buy Andrea's stamp collection if she included her coin collection. [_____] This is not an acceptance. [_____]. Rather, Daniel's reply is a rejection and possibly a counter offer, see below.

WHAT IS IRAC? 101

Rejection and Counter Offer? [_____]

If the offeree expresses to the offeror that he does not want to deal with the offeror, the offer will then be terminated. [_____] Daniel indicated that he would not accept Andrea's offer as proposed, thus he is rejecting her offer to sell stamps. [_____] Andrea's initial offer is dead and may not be reviewed. [_____] Daniel however may have made a counter offer.

Did Daniel make a valid counter offer? [_____]

When an offeree's response to an offer communicates a promise to be bound but only on different terms, it will be construed as a rejection of the offer and a counter offer. [_____] Here, Daniel is promising to be bound but on the sale of both the stamps and coins, different terms. [_____] Daniel's request to buy the stamps and coins for that price indicates definite and certain terms and is communicated to Andrea (again an identifiable offeree), and thus Daniel's is a valid counter offer. [_____]

Acceptance of Counter Offer? [_____]

What is necessary for a valid acceptance is noted above. Here, Andrea said she "would think about it and get back to" Daniel. These are not words that would indicate Andrea intends to exercise the power conferred by Daniel's offer. [_____] Andrea has thus not accepted Daniel's offer. [_____]

Consideration?

Based on the analysis above, there is thus no valid acceptance and no valid contract. If however there had been a valid acceptance, in order to prove a valid contract was formed, there would also need to be evidence of consideration, a bargained-for exchange whereby each party promises to do what the person was not legally obligated to do, or refrain from doing what the person is legally privileged to do. [_____] Here, consideration would be present in the exchange of the stamp collection (and perhaps coin collection) for money, items of value, the giving of which neither party would be obligated to. [_____]

Defenses?

If there were a valid acceptance, because this agreement concerns the sale of goods (a stamp collection) being sold for $15,000, the UCC would govern and the contract would need to be in writing under the statute of frauds to be enforceable. [_____] Here again, from the facts given, the offer appears to have been oral and there was no acceptance. If there had been an acceptance, in order to enforce performance of this contract, it would have had to have been in writing or fall within an exception to the statute of frauds. [_____]

Conclusion

Because Daniel rejected Andrea's offer and made a counter offer which Andrea has not accepted, Daniel and Andrea do not have a binding contract. [_____]

If you are well into 1L, the contracts scenario above should have been straightforward because by now you know this area of law. But, even if you are just starting out, you likely had no problem following the logical flow of the sample answer.

That's what is important to get out of this chapter—just the basic idea that you will be called upon to carefully read new fact patterns, apply the law you will learn to those facts, and reason to logical conclusions. Exams will be more complex than the examples in this chapter, but this gives a sense of the kind of logic required.

Let's do some more practice. Here below are two "mini" essay questions. Try to write answers to both in IRAC (or "IRPC") format. Hint, to answer the first question requires knowledge of a few basic evidence rules and the second a few fundamental rules of civil procedure. If you have not taken these classes or don't know these rules, try to answer anyway imagining what the rule might be (or read the sample answer just through the rules and try to complete the analysis/proof on your own).You are not doing this work for a grade; it is just for exposure to this sort of logical thinking and writing.

QUESTION 1: Priscilla was seriously injured and permanently scarred when Dr. Dagger, who was operating on Priscilla to remove a mole on her chin, slipped and fell slashing Priscilla's

WHAT IS IRAC? 103

cheek. Priscilla sued Dagger for malpractice. At trial, Priscilla called as a witness Nurse Nancy, who was present during Priscilla's surgery. Nancy testified that Dr. Dagger screamed as he slipped, "What the hell is on this damn wet floor? We have to stop the bleeding!" Nancy also testified that just after the surgery, before leaving the operating room, Dagger whispered, "I guess I should not have had that second margarita at lunch." Will Nancy's testimony be admitted at trial?

QUESTION 2: Peter Plaintiff, whose permanent home is in State Y, is serving time in federal prison in State X. Peter holds religious beliefs that prevent him from eating pork. Peter filed an action against State X after a prison guard forced him at gunpoint to eat green eggs and ham on St. Patrick's Day. Peter suffered no monetary damages. Will subject matter jurisdiction be satisfied if Peter brings his action in federal district court in State X?

SAMPLE ANSWER to QUESTION 1

Will Nancy's testimony be admitted at trial?

Relevance

Evidence that has a tendency to prove a fact of consequence to the matter before the court will be deemed relevant. Here, the first part of Nancy's testimony (about what the doctor screamed) might help prove causation of Priscilla's injuries and the second part of her testimony (about his margarita) might help establish fault. All of her testimony is therefore relevant to the action.

Hearsay

Hearsay is an out of court statement, offered to prove the truth of the matter asserted therein. Here, both statements Nancy is testifying about were made in the operating room and therefore out of court. The statements are being offered for truth since the heart of Priscilla's claim would be that the doctor's negligence caused her injuries, and both statements, if true, would help establish that claim. Both statements are therefore hearsay and will not be admitted unless they fall under an exception to the hearsay rule. As discussed below, each statement likely falls under certain exceptions.

Excited Utterance

A hearsay declaration will be admitted pursuant to this exception if it relates to a startling event and is made while the declarant was under the stress caused by the event. Here, slipping while operating on someone would be a startling event. The facts indicate that the doctor "screamed" and cursed as this event occurred. Therefore his first statement: "What the hell..." would qualify as an excited utterance, and would thus be admitted into evidence despite a hearsay objection. The second whispered statement would likely not qualify as an excited utterance as it was quietly stated after the surgery was over, and thus well after the stress of the slip had passed.

Present Sense Impression

A hearsay statement will be admitted pursuant to this exception if the statement describes or explains an event or condition and was made while or immediately after the declarant perceived the event. The doctor's first statement: "What the hell..." would qualify as a present sense impression as he made the statement while or just after slipping, and his statement explained and described the slipping and the bleeding, and would thus be admitted into evidence despite a hearsay objection. It is less clear that the whispered statement would be admitted under this exception, though arguably it does explain that the doctor may have slipped because he was under the influence of alcohol, but, again, this comment was made some time after the slip.

Admission

An admission is an out of court declaration made by a party and offered into evidence against that party. Under the Federal Rules of Evidence, an admission is considered <u>non-hearsay</u>. Here, the doctor's whisper to Nancy about drinking before the surgery was made out of court and is offered against him, likely to prove breach of duty under negligence.

Declaration Against Interest

There is a hearsay exception for declarations against interest but this exception will only apply if the declarant is unavailable. Nothing in the fact pattern indicates that the doctor is

WHAT IS IRAC?

unavailable to testify in this proceeding; therefore this may not qualify as a declaration against interest.

Conclusion

For the reasons discussed above, both statements in Nancy's testimony will likely be admitted into evidence.

SAMPLE ANSWER to QUESTION 2:

Will subject matter jurisdiction be satisfied if Peter brings his action in federal district court in State X?

Subject Matter Jurisdiction

Subject matter jurisdiction ("SMJ") may be established on the basis of federal question or diversity. Diversity jurisdiction requires complete diversity of citizenship and an amount in controversy exceeding $75,000. Here, because Peter ("P") suffered no monetary damages, even if citizenship requirements were met, the court will not have SMJ under diversity jurisdiction since the amount in controversy has not been satisfied. However, as discussed below, the court will likely have federal question jurisdiction.

Federal Question

A claim that arises under the Constitution, laws or treaties of the United States will present a federal question. No minimum amount in controversy is required to establish jurisdiction based on a federal question. Here, P's claim likely raises one or more federal questions: P's being forced to eat ham at gunpoint raises potential violations of both his 1st Amendment freedom of religion rights (about religious dietary restrictions), and his 8th Amendment rights to be free from cruel and unusual punishment. Both of these claims arise under the U.S. Constitution, providing federal questions for the district court to have SMJ. Because there is no amount in controversy requirement for federal question jurisdiction, it poses no problem that P suffered no monetary damages; the fact that his Constitutional rights may have been violated will suffice to raise a federal question.

Conclusion

For the reasons discussed above, the federal district court in State X would have SMJ and the authority to hear P's claims under federal question jurisdiction.

Again, even if you haven't studied the rules needed to answer the mini-essays above, I suspect that the sample responses make sense to you and you see the logical flow.

IRAC-Style Practice—No Need for Legal Knowledge

Below is a sample law school "style" exam to think through. For this question, you do not need any knowledge of the law. In other words, you can complete this in the first months of law school or before law school even starts to get acquainted with the logical thinking process. You can also complete this in your second semester to continue training your organization skills.

Because the "rules" are given in the question, your response if it were graded, would likely be judged on the following criteria: 1) organization/logic, 2) responsiveness to the question, 3) thoroughness (completely answering the question), 4) effective and logical usage of all parts of each applicable rule and all relevant facts, and 5) ability to communicate effectively (including writing in complete sentences).

Sample Question

Adam and five friends, Betty, Carl, David, Ella, and Frank, were soaking in the hot tub at his apartment building, eating fruit and drinking. Adam, Betty, and Carl were drinking virgin margaritas. David and Ella were drinking beer from plastic cups. Frank was sipping a margarita when he saw George walk by the elevator. Frank called to George, "The water is perfect. We've been here almost an hour. Join us!" George immediately jumped into the hot tub. George had nothing to drink.

The hot tub rules state as follows:

- No more than 6 people may be in the hot tub at a time.
- No glass (bottles or drinking glasses).
- No alcohol.

WHAT IS IRAC?

- It is recommended not to remain in hot water for more than 15 minutes.

Did Adam and/or his friends fully comply with the stated rules?

SAMPLE ANSWER *Note: the sample answer below is organized party-by-party, grouping people who were similarly situated. Another logical way to organize this would be rule-by-rule.*

The following response addresses the issues that must be resolved to determine whether the respective parties complied with hot tub rules stated in the fact pattern.

Adam, Betty, and Carl

When they were in the water, before George arrived, Adam, Betty and Carl may have been in compliance with the rules. There were (at that time) no more than six people, and all three were drinking "virgin" or non-alcoholic beverages. The facts do not state whether they were drinking from glass. If they were drinking their virgin margaritas from plastic or Styrofoam (or non-glass) cups, they were in compliance. It does not matter how long they stayed in the water as the 15 minute suggestion was just that, a mere recommendation and not a mandate.

David and Ella

Though there were only six people before George arrived, and though they were drinking from plastic cups, both David and Ella were drinking beer, violating the no alcohol rule. Thus, David and Ella did not comply with the rules.

George

Though he was not drinking anything at the time, because George jumped in with six people already in the tub, George violated the rule regarding occupancy limits.

In conclusion, before George joined them, Abby, Betty, and Carl may well have been in compliance, but for the reasons stated above, David and Ella were not. After George got in the hot tub, all of them were likely in violation of the occupancy limit rule as the facts do not indicate that any of them got out.

END OF SAMPLE ANSWER

Below are additional practice exams that require no knowledge of the law.

Question A

Friday, Patty went to lunch at The Dancer Café ("Café") where she was served a chicken salad sandwich. Later that day, Patty became sick. It was conclusively determined that Patty had food poisoning from salmonella. Patty sued Café Owner and seeks to blame the chefs for negligence.

Dan, Donald, Dalia, and Donna all worked as chefs at Café. Friday, the day Patty ate at Café, Donald and Dalia were working on the vegetable prep line and in sandwich assembly; Dan was responsible for washing dishes and cleaning surfaces as the others filled sandwich orders. On Thursday, the day before Patty ate at Café, Donna prepared duck and chicken. She had them in the oven in a roasting pan for several hours, but did not know the power had gone off after only thirty minutes of cooking. Donna, thinking the poultry was sufficiently cooked, carved the birds, pulled the meat off the bones, put the bones in a soup stock pot, and put the meat in containers in the refrigerator. Donna did not wash the cutting board or knife because she was late and had to leave work. When Dalia got the ticket for Patty's sandwich order on Friday during the lunch rush, Dalia grabbed the nearest cutting board, which turned out to be the one Donna used the day before. Dalia put two slices of bread on the board, spread one slice with mustard and mayonnaise, and layered that slice with lettuce, onion, olives and peppers from the vegetable prep area and chicken salad from a container in the refrigerator. Dalia put the second slice of bread on top of the chicken, grabbed a knife from the counter, sliced and plated the sandwich, and sent it out to the dining room.

The Health Department's rules state in relevant part:

> "Although the risk of salmonella contamination cannot be eliminated, proper preparation and cooking can ensure that poultry is safe for eating. Such proper preparation and cooking requires that: 1) poultry be thoroughly cooked, and that 2) all utensils and surfaces that come in contact with raw poultry must be

WHAT IS IRAC? 109

thoroughly cleaned with hot water and soap before further use."

Did Dan, Donna, Donald and/or Dalia likely violate the poultry preparation and/or cooking rules?

Question B

Sally, age 20, Hal age 17, and Steven age 27 entered a pie-eating contest. The rules for the contest are as follows:

- No hands can be used.
- The first person to finish their whole pie and to then stand up will be declared the winner!
- In the event of a tie—more than one first place winner will be selected.
- Any visible signs of sickness will cause disqualification, and
- All contestants must complete and sign a registration form with a liability waiver before the contest starts; children under 18 must also have a parent or guardian present and have a parent or guardian sign their registration form.

All three, Sally, Hal, and Steven completed registration agreements including signing the waiver. As soon as the judges said, "Go," Sally sat down to a big spoonful of strawberry pie. Sally quickly shoveled spoon after spoon in her mouth finishing the whole pie, and jumping up before any other contestant. Sally felt sick to her stomach and ready to vomit but hid this well.

When he heard the "Go" signal, Hal scooped forkfuls of pecan pie into his mouth relishing every bite. A few crumbs spilled which he quickly brushed off his face with his hands. Hal finished eating his pie at the exact same time Sally did, and Hal yelled "WooHoo, I can't believe I ate the whole thing!" Immediately thereafter, Hal vomited.

Steven, with his hands clasped behind his back, dove face first into a chocolate pudding pie. Working slowly and steadily, Steven licked every bit of filling and crust, finishing several minutes after Sally and Hal, standing and smiling with satisfaction. Steven was certain he did not win because the others ate faster than he did, but he thoroughly enjoyed each bite and had fun. Who will likely win the contest and why?

Question C

Jimmy and Timmy entered a music video contest.

Jimmy submitted a 5-minute video of a song inspired by an old Elton John tune. Jimmy is seen in the video seated atop his grandfather's oak desk, singing and playing guitar. Jimmy created the video originally as a love song for his girlfriend, who immediately told Jimmy he should use the video as a submission to the contest. Jimmy did not particularly want to enter a contest but uploaded the video simply to please his girlfriend.

Timmy submitted a 4-minute and 60-second video of a song Timmy believed he himself had made up. Timmy cut the video in his picturesque backyard, with a 5-second fade in and fade out showing his yard at the beginning and end of the video. Timmy is seen singing and playing harmonica. Timmy created the video for the contest and uploaded it as directed to the contest site on a bright, bright, sunshiny day. He was certain he would win. Timmy played the song for his guitar teacher who immediately said that the lyrics were almost identical to a song composed by Johnny Nash and first recorded in 1972.

Relevant contest rules require that all videos must:

- feature someone seated at a desk;
- be the original work of the contestant (covers will not be accepted);
- be created specifically for this contest (videos that were submitted to this contest in previous years or any other contest or competition will not be accepted);
- be a maximum of five minutes in length; and
- be uploaded to the contest site.

Will Jimmy and/or Timmy be found to have complied with contest rules?

WHAT IS IRAC? 111

Question D

Abby, Bob, and Cal were on an airplane flying on a redeye flight from Fort Lauderdale to a conference in Los Angeles. They were seated in aisle 14, in seats D, E, and F respectively. About 30 minutes before arrival at LAX, a flight attendant made the following announcement regarding landing rules: "In preparation for landing, all passengers must fasten their seatbelts, place their seats in the upright position, stow their tray tables, and stow all large electronics."

Abby and Bob had fallen asleep during the flight. Cal spent the flight watching in-flight movies on his laptop (using ear buds to hear the movies). Abby woke just before landing and spoke briefly with Cal. Bob did not wake until the plane landed.

Just after the landing preparation announcement described above was made, a flight attendant came by to check aisle 14.

Before she fell asleep, Abby had been eating a sandwich on her open tray table. Abby never touched the button that controlled the position of her seat. Abby traveled with a tablet and iPhone; she left her laptop at home.

Cal's movie was interrupted by the announcement, which Cal heard and immediately pushed the button on the side of his seat that controls the reclined or upright position of the seat.

Bob fell asleep with his computer on his lap. The computer was closed, in its case, and covered the entire flight by a blanket Bob used to stay warm while he slept.

Which if any of the passengers discussed above will be found in compliance with airplane landing rules?

CHAPTER 12

DAILY HABITS

Classmates and professors will remember you. How do you want them to see you (and how do you see yourself) now and as a future lawyer?

My guess is you want to be known as someone reliable, someone who takes deadlines seriously, returns calls and reads e-mails carefully and responds promptly, arrives on time, keeps appointments, and effectively manages your calendar.

To be licensed to practice law you must know the applicable ethical rules, but to be *successful* for a lifetime, you must also act in a professional manner. That starts in law school if not beforehand.

The Rules of Professional Responsibility that you will study in law school provide a floor not a ceiling. You will want to do more than just follow written rules, including (and perhaps first and foremost), earning and keeping people's trust.

Everyone you meet and/or work with now—your classmates, friends, family, and colleagues—is a potential referral source. Make sure they would want to refer you!

I recall a college classmate who cheated on an exam and later went to law school. If I am ever asked to refer that classmate for a case or job opportunity, I won't. As you complete the following reflection, think about people you trust and those you don't—and why.

PIF Reflection:

1. List two people you know you would trust in the future. What past acts or qualities make them people you would trust?

> 2. List two people you know you would not trust in the future. What past acts or qualities make them people you would not trust?

A highly successful professional gave me the following career advice: during or right after every work or volunteer experience, (every case, project, conference, etc.), note in a confidential file for yourself the names of people you worked with and actions they took that you appreciated and those you did not appreciate. You would be surprised how many people come back around in your life. It is cliché to say the world is small, but it is true. And, the legal world is even smaller.

Your private lists will help you remember how people acted and whether or not you want to work with them again, and whether you trust them or not. You would also be surprised how many people keep lists; make sure your behavior puts you on their "want to work with again" positive lists.

Note: Being ethical and professional does *not* mean never making mistakes. Having served on faculty honor code committees for decades, I have seen students come forth immediately to report themselves after inadvertently committing a violation. Often, these matters were treated as good-faith errors and quickly resolved. In contrast, students who tried to hide or cover up alleged violations were often found culpable and ended up facing far more serious consequences than had they initially admitted wrongdoing.

The same is often true in practice. Lawyers make mistakes. (Why do you think they call it the *practice* of law?) Most mistakes are correctable. But you have to have your antennae up so that you realize when you or those you work with make mistakes, and you must be willing to and have the courage to speak up about such errors. Then, you have to figure out how best to fix them and take steps to do so in a timely fashion.

Communicate Respectfully and in a Timely Manner

The points below are by no means exhaustive; they are just a few useful observations and things to think about:

- Write and send respectful e-mails and texts.
- Address your professors and law school administrators and staff with their appropriate titles unless they invite you to use their first names.
- Professors are often your best references for first law jobs, so be polite when writing to them—and don't write them during class.
- Don't fire off angry texts or emails. Write what angers or frustrates you for yourself, without sending, then see if there are alternate ways to resolve issues. (Think about the old saying, "You catch more flies with honey than with vinegar.")
- Don't be too quick to hit *Send*. If at all possible, keep texts and emails as drafts overnight or at least a few hours and re-read with fresh eyes before sending. You may be under a lot of stress and may not catch typos or inappropriate wording or tone.
- Do not send messages you may later regret. (Ask yourself how you will feel re-reading this 6 months from now.)
- There is nothing wrong with asking your professor thoughtful questions, or even challenging professors, but do so politely and in a professional manner. And, try to answer questions yourself, such as by carefully reading the syllabus, before reaching out to ask your professor.

Read Messages from Your Law School

Most law school administrators and faculty still communicate by e-mail, but many law students do not. The disconnect is troubling. Students often miss a great deal that the people sending messages assume was read and understood. Get in the habit of reading your e-mail. You don't need to read it immediately, so you can turn off notifications that disturb your focus. Just dedicate some daily time, maybe first thing in the morning or late in the evening when you are too tired to study, and read everything that isn't junk.

You may find messages about registration deadlines or scholarship opportunities. And it can be embarrassing and make you look less competent when you ask professors or administrators about things that have already been clearly communicated in e-mails. Law schools spend extensive time and energy setting up programs to help students succeed, yet faculty and administrators often express how difficult it is to get students to attend events, even when food is offered. How many students do not attend because they did not read the e-mail?

Messages Sent Are Not Always Received or Read

It is too often assumed that messages sent are received and read accurately. But e-mails often end up in spam folders, texts are missed, and some messages simply are never read (or not read carefully) by the intended recipients. As a professional, make it your business to answer all messages that call for replies. If you do not have time for a thoughtful response, send a brief acknowledgment noting that you received the correspondence and will reply as soon as possible. Then calendar the date to follow up so you respond fully when you say you will. When someone requests that you do something, send a reply noting when the task has been completed. If you sent an important email to someone else, check back politely with that person if you have not received a reply within a reasonable amount of time. (What is "reasonable" may differ with different people and in different contexts, so ask a trusted mentor for advice if you are unsure of when to follow up.)

Return Calls and E-Mails Promptly

As a professional, make a habit of returning messages as promptly as possible. Don't leave people hanging. If you don't know something or need more time, indicate that and then be sure to get back to the person when you say you will. This is an important habit now and for dealing with colleagues and clients in the future. Lack of responsiveness and lack of communication are factors cited frequently by dissatisfied clients. Don't let that be you.

Be Careful What You Post on Social Media

Employers *will* look. Act accordingly. (When in doubt, don't post.) Posting something illegal may affect your moral character application (and possibly worse). Posting something immoral or even in bad taste, can influence your professional reputation. Be careful. That said, do post accomplishments that reflect well on you, such as placing in a moot-court competition or being selected for a school honor. Talk with professionals in your law school's career services office if you are in doubt about whether to post something, and about how to effectively use social media to create your own brand and promote your positive reputation.

Be Organized

Back up your data. Keep lists. Organize documents into files and folders in a logical way so that you can easily retrieve them. (For the bar exam and possibly future jobs, you may need access to transcripts, records of jobs you have had with your supervisors' names and contact information, a list of addresses you have had, and copies of recommendation letters.)

Did I say, "Be sure to back up your data." (I know I did.) Back up in the cloud or somewhere separate from your device in case it is lost or stolen.)

Meet Deadlines, Be on Time, and Comply with Rules

Complying with deadlines and rules, and being punctual are critical for successful professionals, especially a lawyer. They are habits that you can cement (or begin) during law school and bar prep. While it may seem obvious that lawyers must comply with deadlines, students frequently miss them, and faculty nationwide regularly lament the numbers of students who turn work in late without even requesting extensions. If you arrive late to court (without notifying the clerk), or you miss a hearing without requesting and receiving an extension (and typically having good cause), your client could lose a home, custody of children, or even their liberty. And, even when such actions do not have any negative consequences for clients, your colleagues will notice and remember.

At every turn, you are creating your reputation—either enhancing or diminishing it. People remember when you are rude, late, or don't meet deadlines.

This may be hard to believe, but people regularly fail bar exams because they do not upload their answers on time. Some are not even allowed to sit for the exam because they arrive late to the testing site. Other applicants are kicked out during the exam because they bring in forbidden items or wear prohibited clothing. All of these are preventable by simply reading the information and notices from bar examiners. Start in 1L making a habit of carefully studying and complying with law school rules.

> **PIF Reflection: Calendaring**
>
> Throughout law school, bar prep, and your professional career, you will have many dates to remember, including when applications are due to avoid late fees. Calendaring seems so simple but many a malpractice action stems from missed deadlines that cause harm to clients. Start now if you don't have a system in place.
>
> - Do you calendar all upcoming appointments, deadlines, and meetings?
>
> - Do you have a reminder system?
>
> - How do you feel when you go to the doctor and have to wait more than 30 minutes?

Chapter 13

Exams

Though many try to cloak 1L in all sorts of mystery, the "secrets" to law school exam success are pretty straightforward:

- Know and understand the legal rules and principles your professor will test.
- Read critically—and train your critical reading skills daily.
- Understand the logic behind IRAC or other exam writing formats.
- Learn multiple choice strategies if you will be tested in part in that manner.
- Take practice tests under timed conditions, self-assess with sample answers, and work to steadily and continuously improve the quality of your responses.

In a previous chapter, we talked about IRAC generally. Here, we'll look at both essays and multiple-choice questions and discuss some exam taking strategies and tips, and provide suggestions on how to self-assess your answers to practice exams.

The most effective way to learn and retain what you need to know for exams is to continuously build one day at a time, one week at a time: read, learn, and outline throughout the first months. Then ramp up weaving in practice exams as you get closer to finals. Your goals when you walk into each final should be to know the rules needed to analyze issues that arise in each topic area within the subjects your professor said may be tested and how to approach analyzing those rules when applied to new sets of facts. You need to see the big picture (the subject as a whole) and individual sub-areas as wholes—then you must also know the details such as interpretations of and exceptions to particular parts of rules within each sub-area. For example, in Torts, you will want to organize the course into topics such as

Intentional Torts, Negligence, Product-Related Liability, and Privacy/Economic Torts. You will want to know that Negligence, often the most heavily tested area, breaks down into the following "big" categories based on the elements: duty, breach, causation, damages. You also want to know the defenses that can be asserted and their effect on the outcome of a dispute. And, then for each of these sub-areas, you will want to know very detailed rules and exceptions of rules. (Check out the lists in my *Step-by-Step Guide to Torts* for examples of both big picture and detailed rules.)

If you will be tested with closed book exams, then you will want to train your memorization skills. In this smartphone age, our memories have taken the back seat. We don't need them much, if at all. But you will need instant recall on exams.

Mnemonics are memory-aid techniques that have likely been helping people since ancient times. They can be verbal—perhaps a key acronym, word, or poem that helps you remember something. Memory tips can be in song form. They can be based on lists, and the easiest to memorize are lists of three. They can also be visual, such as associating arrows to recall how one concept stems from or links to another.

Where to Get Practice Tests?

Ask your law librarian or ASP faculty, and consult the resources from reliable legal publishers.

Essay Exams

First, let's walk through the actions you'll take to answer an essay question—next we'll get into the strategic thinking behind the process.

Carefully read all instructions and know how many points each part of the exam is worth. Allocate your time in proportion to the points possible for respective portions of the exam.

With an individual question, start at the end of the fact pattern with the "call" of the question. That's what you must answer, so begin there. Then read the fact pattern. Then reread the call of the question.

Read slowly and carefully, touching each word and mumbling it aloud under your breath, circling and highlighting

EXAMS

key words. Take notes. Jot down (on paper or start a "notes" section at the end of your draft answer file), any words that raise "discussable issues" (more on issue spotting below). As part of note-taking, you might create a quick chronology, listing key facts in the order in which they occur. Essays often tell the factual "story" out of order so chronologies can be especially helpful.

- For example, in a torts negligence fact pattern for which you are analyzing proximate cause, tracking the chain of causation requires knowing what happened and when. Looking at your own ordered list of events on scratch paper or in a notes section of your draft answer, you will readily see if an event came between the defendant's actions and the victim's injury. You can then assess that intervening event to determine if it was foreseeable or not, and complete your proximate cause discussion. (This will make sense after studying torts.)

- Another example is a contracts question in which there are numerous communications between the buyer and seller or between the employer and employee. In order to know the legal significance of each communication, you may need to know exactly what was communicated, and when. (Remember this when you learn something called the "mailbox rule").

Next, create an exam outline. (This is different from your course outline.) Think of your exam outline as a table of contents to your essay answer. Include the main discussable issues and possibly relevant sub issues, organized into a logical order (often, but not always, tracking the calls of the question). If you type your outline into your essay answer file, you can often turn your outline into your actual answer.

For example, a question asks, "Of what crimes, if any, may the defendant be convicted?" Your main points in your outline (that can be turned into headings in your actual answer) could be each of the crimes you intend to discuss. In a torts question involving multiple parties, the headings may be the various lawsuits: *A v. B, B v. C*, etc. In a contracts question, your answer may be organized in a chronological manner, tracking the offer, acceptance, etc. for each potential breach of contract claim.

Then, write a full and complete logical answer. You can use an IRAC style unless something else is recommended. (See earlier chapter discussing IRAC.) While it may not always matter *how* you conclude or "who wins" on an essay, it is important to conclude. Two well-written essay answers may reach opposite conclusions—especially when the facts are "gray," meaning there are good arguments on both sides. It is also possible to conclude in the alternative. (For example, *Based on the foregoing analysis, the defendant will* likely *be found to have possessed the intent to kill the victim here. If, however, the prosecution is unable to prove intent to kill, the prosecution may well be able to demonstrate that the defendant possessed the intent to cause serious bodily harm or that at the very least the defendant's actions showed a reckless indifference to human life.*)

So to recap, the process involves three steps, 1) read critically beginning with the call of the question, 2) outline, 3) write. Let's look deeper, starting with critical reading.

Exam reading includes careful reading and deep engagement with the material, *analyzing and thinking* while you read. It can help to superimpose a mental template (issues and rules in a logical structure) on top of the words so that you immediately see their significance and begin reasoning them into a logical order. (You can see examples of the basic logical order of frequently tested areas in contracts, torts, and criminal law in my West *Step-by-Step Guides.*)

When you read exam questions, read with a stylus if reading on screen or a pencil or pen if reading on paper. Circle or underline key words. Circle party names the first time they are introduced in a fact pattern. Circle the connecting words *and* and *or*.

Underline the call(s) of the question (also called the interrogatory/ies) so you know exactly what you are answering. Do not answer questions that were not asked. (For example, if a tort question asks, Discuss any and all possible intentional torts," you would not discuss negligence.)

EXAMS

Lean forward and sit up straight when you read. Read with three senses: touch, sight, and hearing. *Point* to each word with your finger or pencil (touching the screen or paper) while you *read* with your eyes, and at the same time softly *say* the words aloud under your breath. (This is called subvocalization.) You will not miss words or zone out while reading this way.

Most important, *think* while you read. Ask yourself *why* each word in the fact pattern is there.

In essay exam answers, you will *use* facts to prove or disprove elements of identifiable causes of action, crimes, defenses, or other legal theories. But unless you know and understand the law well enough, you will not readily see the significance of words you are reading.

When you know the law well, reading certain facts will trigger rules in your mind. You will flag these facts by circling, underlining, or highlighting any word or words that appear to raise possible questions that could potentially be analyzed and resolved. (This is *issue spotting*.) In your answer, you will then use the facts to prove or disprove the elements of the rules, as we discussed in the earlier chapter on IRAC.

If you see the words, "break," "breaking," or "broken" in a criminal law question, you will immediately think that burglary might be at issue. And, if you are reading a torts question and see the words "defective" next to a ladder or food processor, you will recall rules regarding products liability.

Suppose you are reading a criminal law fact pattern and see that the defendant was diagnosed with schizophrenia. You would immediately underline the word *schizophrenia* and jot in the margin something like "Insanity defense?" Why? All of the tests for insanity require that the defendant "suffer from a mental disease or defect," so although this one word does not necessarily mean that insanity is a *discussable* issue, it may be, and you need to be alert to the possibility. The word "schizophrenia" is therefore an issue trigger for a possible insanity defense analysis.

If a criminal law fact pattern indicated a defendant was engaged in some other crime at the time a death resulted, what might that suggest? After you have finished homicide in criminal law you will recognize immediately that is a tip-off that felony murder might be a discussable issue. Again, you might ultimately conclude that the felony murder rule does not apply, perhaps what happened did not amount to a "dangerous felony" or the rule is inapplicable for some other reason. But the very fact (a death occurring during the course of another crime) is a hint (trigger or tip) that felony murder may be a relevant and discussable issue.

On a criminal procedure (crim pro) exam, the minute you see a fact pattern involving "police" and a suspect who "blurted out" something, you would sense that *Miranda* might be at issue. (And, spoiler alert: to provide an adequate answer on a law school crim pro essay, you must thoroughly understand the Miranda rule itself and its many exceptions; you cannot just be familiar with the TV version.)

Remember, on law exams, *it is often just as important to recognize that a rule is implicated even if ultimately it is not established or proven under the given facts. In other words, you can earn just as many points analyzing why the moving party will not win as you might earn in a discussion where you find the moving party prevails.*

The main point of law school essay testing is typically not to advocate for one "winner." It is to show that you understand what questions (issues) the facts give rise to, and, given the law you learned during the semester and clearly articulated in your answer, how and why the facts from the exam question tend to prove or disprove each element of those rules.

Torts Issue Trigger Quiz

Keep lists of "trigger" terms for every subject you are studying. Test yourself quickly here below: what cause of action, rule, or theory do you think of when you see the following words in a torts fact pattern?

1. Extreme and outrageous
2. Rescue
3. Child

4. Premises

5. Product

While every essay differs and professors' styles differ, there are some parallels in essay exams. These tips should be applicable in most instances. As always, though, follow any specific guidance that your professors offer. They will be grading your exams, so follow their lead and give them what they want. (The same will be true in practice of judges. Different courtrooms will have different rules and customs.) Bottom line: *know your audience.*

General Essay Tips

- Answer the questions asked. Many students waste time on non-issues. If you have time after completing an analysis of everything specifically requested and the issues you know must be resolved to answer the questions asked, by all means write about other areas that you think might be at issue. Read carefully and give your professors what they ask for.

- Approach essays as follows: (1) read the interrogatory and then read the facts. Then reread the interrogatory; (2) read every word using three senses, read with your eyes, aloud under your breath, and touch each word with your pencil, pen, finger, or stylus.

- Slow down. Expect that some of your classmates will be typing while you are still reading the question and outlining your answer. Do not let that throw you. Make certain *you* understand what is and what is not asked of you, and see how the facts fit the analytical steps of resolving the specific question or questions *before* you write your answer.

- Before you write, organize and outline. At a minimum, your outlining goal should be to note the main headings (and subheadings) you will include in your answer. There is often more than one logical way to organize. For example, you might organize a torts answer by party, lawsuit, or cause of action; a contract answer by communication or event; or a criminal law essay by crime or by defendant where there are multiple defendants. Any systematic, logical organization is usually fine.

- Allocate your time so that you answer all parts of the questions, if there is more than one interrogatory or if the interrogatory poses a multipart question. Generally, the more facts that relate to a particular issue, the more time you should spend writing about that.

- Cross out words in the fact pattern after you write about the issues they raise in your answer. Look back at the fact pattern periodically while you are typing your answer to see if there are words you have not crossed out. Might they be useful? Why? Do they raise new issues? Do they bolster arguments in support of or against issues you have already analyzed?

- Try to use as many facts as possible. Do not provide a summary of the facts at the beginning of your essay; *use* the facts *within* the analysis or "proof" section of your answer to prove or disprove elements of rules of law. Sometimes, law professors will include "red herrings" or facts that have no bearing on the problem but most facts are in the question for a reason. So, *think about* each fact to see if it triggers an issue, and include it in your analysis/argument if it supports or refutes some element of a rule of law, or otherwise affects some relevant argument (perhaps a policy argument). If you quote from the question, do so selectively and use quotation marks.

- Write in a way that clearly spells out your reasoning and logic. Write with grammatically correct language, but don't try to sound eloquent. Keep it simple and straightforward.

- Focus on the most serious issues first (unless you are writing in another *logical* order, such as chronological order where appropriate). For example, if someone has battered a victim, and that victim *dies* as a result of the battery, start with the homicidal offenses before mentioning battery (if that is even relevant). Likewise, write about a lesser included offense within the larger crime; for example, if there is a larceny and robbery, discuss a robbery first, and write about the larceny within the discussion of the robbery, since the larceny elements are essentially "subsets" of the robbery elements. (This will make sense after you study criminal law.)

- Write in complete sentences, thoroughly analyzing the facts to resolve the issues. Bullet points can sometimes be helpful, such as when noting a list. But, don't expect your professor to follow your shorthand. Fully "spell out" your thinking.

- Provide a key to any terms or party names that you abbreviate. For example, if you abbreviate "contract" with the symbol "K," write *"contract (K)" or "contract (hereinafter 'K')"* the first time you use that abbreviation. You might think this association is so obvious that it's unnecessary to identify it, but the abbreviation "K" is also used to mean "$1,000," so even something so seemingly straightforward may be misconstrued.

- Avoid hammering one point of view. Essays are about analysis not advocacy. Each issue may lend itself to both a defense and plaintiff/prosecution perspective, as the facts can and frequently do cut both ways. If you get stuck trying to advocate in a manner that's too one-sided, you may miss points to be gained from analyzing the opposing party's perspective. Note: If you write about two opposing arguments, conclude your thoughts by noting which side has the stronger position *and why* before moving on to your next area of discussion.

- Write complete (but succinct) rule statements, and then prove up (analyze) each element of each rule—piece by piece. Lawyers break complex thoughts down into logical parts. Elements are components of the bundle that is a rule, and each part must be proved. This is also true for defenses, as defense theories often have multiple elements that must be discussed. (Always consider defenses when analyzing crimes or causes of action.) Know the difference between tests that include *factors* (all of which need not always be established but are typically balanced) and *elements* (each of which must be proven by the requisite level of proof).

- Type neatly. If you don't type well, take typing lessons and practice before final exams. If you are handwriting, make sure your writing is legible. (If the professor can't easily read what you write, they might not award points for your thoughts.)

- Write using lawyerly language. I do not mean that you should use formal, ritualistic language such "the party of the first part heretofore contends . . ."). I mean that you should write in a clear and professional manner. For example:

    o   Do write: *For these reasons, the plaintiff is unlikely to prevail.* (Do **not** write: *The plaintiff's argument is really not going to fly.*)

    o   Do write: *While it may be possible for the plaintiff to prevail, for the reasons stated above, it appears that the defendant has the stronger argument here.* (Do **not** write: *This is a wash. It is up to the jury. The jurors could decide either way here.*)

- Avoid writing in the first person (do not use "I" or "we"). On exams, it doesn't matter what you *think* or what you *believe*. What matters is whether the facts prove, or fail to prove, the legal theories you have articulated.

Please don't be offended by this. Your opinions do matter *outside of exams*. Write personal thoughts in private journals and in the margins of your casebook; talk about your views with classmates and professors in office hours. Just leave them out of exams. You are not training to be an op ed writer. Judges will not care about your opinion but about the facts of your client's case and the legal rules, policies, and procedures.

- Do write: *For the reasons stated above, the defendant will likely prevail.* (Do **not** write: *I think the defendant will win.*)

- Do write: *After weighing the facts on both sides and for the reasons stated above, it appears that the plaintiff has the stronger argument on this question because the plaintiff has more evidence and that evidence is more credible.* (Do **not** write: *I believe the plaintiff has the better argument.*)

- Do write: *The defendant's spitting on the plaintiff/victim is an offensive action. Reasonable people find spitting to be a rude and even demeaning gesture.* Do **not** write: *The defendant's spitting on the plaintiff/victim is offensive. I would be horrified if someone spat on me that way.*

Proofread—Aloud Under Your Breath, if Possible

If you have time to proofread do so before you upload a final exam. While re-reading your answer, you will also see if what you wrote was logical, clear, and responsive, meaning you answered the question(s) asked.

Make Sure to Close the Books

If your final exam will be closed book, practice essays should be closed book. Force yourself to answer the questions as fully as you can, without looking anything up. Only *after* you finish to the best of your ability should you study the sample or model answers, self-assess, and look up rules you do not know or understand.

Self-Assess Your Essay Writing

After completing a practice essay, look carefully at your own answer and a reliable sample answer. Sit with both. How are they the same and how do they differ? Pay attention to content, organization, phrasing, and presentation. Note how precise and complete the rule statements are. Are there any rules you can learn more about or rule statements you can memorize more thoroughly? What about proof (application/analysis)? Is there proof of the existence or lack thereof of each element of each rule at issue? Was every key fact used? Review your answer and the sample answer side by side, and, as a clever detective:

- look for what the sample included that your answer did not contain, and what you may have written about that was not in the sample answer;
- be sure you understand *why* the sample answer included what was discussed and why the sample answer left out things you may have thought were important;
- look at the sample answer for content, organization, and style, and make sure your answer is reader friendly!;
- look at the rules stated in the sample answer and be sure you understand them; and
- reread the fact pattern and then look at how the facts were used in discussing each issue in the sample answer.

Then, after your general compare-and-contrast, ask these specific questions:

[ ] Did I finish within the allotted time?

[ ] Did I spot the main discussable issues? (And did I see which issues were major and required more discussion, and which were minor and called for less emphasis?)

[ ] Did I state the rules correctly?

EXAMS 131

- [ ] Did I use facts to show why (to *prove*) each element of each rule was or was not established in the question?
- [ ] Did I reason to a logical conclusion for every main issue I raised?
- [ ] Was my answer presented in a manner that was organized and easy to read?

After you have done this first part of self-assessing, find concrete ways to improve. The examples below are illustrations. Your situation is unique to you. The key is to figure out where you need to improve and to then create a doable plan of action for your success. Make every effort to leave each practice session with at least two specific ideas about how you can improve.

Improvement Action Items

Check the items that apply to you.

- [ ] I must read the questions more carefully. In upcoming exams, I will read the call of the question first, then read the facts, and then reread the call of the question before I begin outlining. I will also underline the call of the question, and I will keep the fact pattern and my outline in front of me as I write my answer.
- [ ] I need to manage my time better. (I wrote too long on the first question and had little time for the next question.) Know how long you will have for each of the questions on your final exam and practice your timing. Be sure to allocate time to read and outline before you write and to proofread before you finish.

    > *Note from the author: Time and time again, I have seen students improve grades significantly when they get into the habit of spending more time reading, thinking, and outlining* **before** *writing.*

- [ ] I must type faster. (I have the thoughts in my head, but don't get them out fast enough.) I will work on improving my typing skills.
- [ ] I need to understand the law better. (I either did not see issues or I saw what the issues were but did not write

applicable rule statements clearly.) I will work to find different ways of studying that give me a deeper understanding of the rules of law. For example, I might read a hornbook in addition to the casebook.

[ ] I'm not using enough facts. Cross out words from the fact pattern as you use them in your answer. Learn the law more thoroughly. The better your knowledge of the law, the better your ability to quickly see how these new facts prove or disprove elements of governing rules.

Self-Assessment: Your Turn to Self-Assess

1. Did I finish the entire essay within the allotted time? [ ] Yes [ ] No
Improvement action:

2. Did I spot and write about the main issues? [ ] Yes [ ] No
Improvement action:

3. Did I allocate my time well as I was writing? (Did I write too much on any one issue such that I gave short shrift to other issues?) [ ] Yes [ ] No
Improvement action:

4. Did I state the rules correctly and succinctly? [ ] Yes [ ] No
Improvement action:

5. Did I use facts to show why each element of each rule was or was not established in the question? [ ] Yes [ ] No
Improvement action:

6. Did I reason to a logical conclusion for every main issue I raised? [ ] Yes [ ] No
Improvement action:

EXAMS

7. Was my answer presented in a manner that was organized and easy to read? [ ] Yes [ ] No

Improvement action:

Bottom line: Practice before finals. The more practice exams you take, the more opportunities you will have to learn and improve. And, this does not happen in one sitting but slowly and surely over a number of weeks (or months). As you practice, a useful tool can sometimes be to study fact patterns and sample answers, and then work backward. In other words, *outline the answer*. Ask yourself what you would have needed in an outline to produce this sort of answer. Then look *back* to the facts to see how and where the answer got its analysis out of these particular facts. How did this answer use the facts selected to reason to certain conclusions? Usually we move from question to answer. But turning that process around, and moving from answer (end goal) back to the question, can sometimes help you see more clearly where you need to focus.

Self-Talk and Practice Tests

What do you tell yourself after you complete a practice test? Do you say, "Making this mistake now will help me not to make it on the actual final exam; making mistakes now is a good thing," and pat yourself on the back? Or do you complete a practice test, look at the results, and say, "How could I be so stupid as to miss *that?*"

If the latter, stop the critical voice. Rephrase. You are not stupid. You are learning. And if you keep learning, you are indeed extremely smart! The problem is not making mistakes—it's not learning from them! Watch what you tell yourself. Keep the expectation that you will succeed front and center always, in everything you do, say, and think. You must self-assess and work to improve. Nowhere is it written that you are supposed to know it all without working at it.

Multiple Choice Questions

Some law faculty test with multiple-choice questions (MCQs). If so, you may want to practice with those as well. Here is one way to approach answering MCQs on law exams:

- Cover the answer choices so you don't get suckered into selecting a seductive-looking answer before you even know the facts, and so that you do not become biased while reading the facts.

- Next, read the interrogatory or "call of the question," at or near the end of the facts. This might help determine which area within the course the question is testing. For example, if it's a contract question that is testing formation, that may help to rule out answer choices dealing with damages.

- Then read the fact pattern *and reread the interrogatory*. Remember to use active reading strategies: read with a stylus or pencil in hand, touching and mumbling each word to yourself as you read. Underline words that trigger legal issues. Based on the law, reason through the facts to draw a conclusion that you believe best answers the precise question asked.

- Only after completing these steps (including carefully rereading the interrogatory) should you then take your hand off the answer choices and read through the first choice carefully, asking yourself: "Is this choice plausible?" "Is it responsive to the question?" "Does it mirror the answer I reasoned to?" "Is it even a correct statement in and of itself?" If the choice contains an incorrect rule statement, does not answer the question asked, or answers it incorrectly (applies the law incorrectly to these specific facts), immediately put a line through it and go on to the next choice.

- Ask yourself the same questions regarding each of the remaining answer choices, crossing out any that are wrong or don't answer the question. Do this clearly so that you don't mistakenly think an answer choice is still on the table if you have ruled it out. (Some people find it helpful to play a sort of "find the wrong answers" game with themselves. The more you rule out, the better. If you like puzzles, this might be a good strategy for you.)

- Now, what are you left with? If only one answer choice remains, select that one and quickly move on to the next question. If you have two answer choices that are both consistent with your conclusion but for different reasons, read each one again carefully and isolate what exactly differs between the two choices. Then see if one includes faulty reasoning, an internal inconsistency, an incorrect rule statement, or fails to answer the exact question posed. Reread the interrogatory to be sure you understand the exact question. Reread the facts as necessary. By process of elimination, choose the best of the remaining answers.

- Note that the best answer might not be perfect. Select the answer that seems to reason to the best conclusion when applying appropriate law to resolve the issue asked in the particular question.

After you complete practice tests, assess your work using the suggestions and reflection charts below or using a different system that you develop or one that your professor or ASP faculty suggests. Do what works for you. But, use assessment information *to improve. Don't spend even one minute being down on yourself or frustrated by the fact that you got the wrong answers.* That's a waste of time. Practice tests are learning opportunities; with each practice question you complete, you gain a better understanding of certain rules, your reading skills become more refined, and your reasoning more strategic. (Completing practice tests is like weight lifting; train consistently and you will get stronger.)

Below are some of the common places people make mistakes in MCQs.

Reading error?

If you read part of an MCQ incorrectly, ask yourself why.

- Did you read too fast?
- Did you drift off while reading?
- Did you assume some fact that was not in the fact pattern?

- Did you not understand the meaning of one or more words that turned out to affect the entire question?
- If a reading error, which part of the question did you read incorrectly: the call, the facts, or the answer choices? (And, again, why did you miss that part? Were you rushing? Nervous? Overconfident?)

Once you know why you missed a question, you can then take steps to change the behavior. Reading incorrectly is one of the most common reasons for error and the easiest mistake to fix. Remember your critical reading skills, and use the method I've repeatedly suggested in this book: **touch** each word *and* **say** it aloud under your breath *as you* **read** with your eyes. It works.

<u>Didn't know or understand a rule?</u>

If you can see that you did not know or understand the rule required to answer the question, go look it up and either write it in your outline or flash cards, or say it out loud several times, or both. (If you want to be sure you understand it, try explaining the concept to someone else.)

<u>Didn't finish in time?</u>

If your professor tells you that you will have ten multiple choice questions to complete in 20 minutes, you know you have two minutes per question. So, practice under timed conditions. If you don't finish in time, ask yourself why.

- Are you timing yourself?
- Did you lose time by focusing too long on one question? If you get stuck, guess and move on, then return to the question if you have extra time when you've completed the set of MCQs.
- Did you drift off while reading?
- Did you get distracted?

Each set of practice questions is an opportunity to incrementally improve your accuracy, speed, and your ability to focus for longer and more concentrated periods of time.

EXAMS

Multiple Choice Reflection #1—Wrong Answers

Check all boxes that apply when you got the question wrong:

[ ] I read the question (the interrogatory) incorrectly.

[ ] I missed a key word or words in the fact pattern.

[ ] I read one or more answer choices incorrectly.

[ ] I didn't understand what the question was asking, or I didn't see the issue.

[ ] I didn't know the law that I needed to apply to the issue to reason to a conclusion.

[ ] I knew the rule, but I didn't understand the underlying principles the question was testing (so I narrowed it down to two possible choices, but I missed the best one).

[ ] I knew the correct answer, but I entered it incorrectly.

Multiple Choice Reflection #2—Right Answers

Complete this reflection as you review questions you got right:

Question # ___

[ ] I understand why I chose the answer I chose.

[ ] I chose the correct answer for the right reason.

Note: If you chose the right answer for the wrong reason, write out here why your reasoning was flawed:

_____
_____

Rules/concepts tested in this question and tips to remember this area of questioning in the future:

_____
_____

Ramp up for Finals

During finals, you must cocoon. In those last weeks and days, it must be all study and self-care, which includes sufficient sleep, exercise, and good nutrition/hydration. Learn to be "self-centered" in a good way, in a way that allows for success. If you want company or need a study break, do what it takes to ensure that these breaks are positive and uplifting. Avoid any negative thing or person, as much as possible.

For many of you, this part will be extremely difficult. Others will get in the way—intentionally or accidentally. Distractions and procrastination enticements will come in every shape and size. You may feel guilty spending so much time on yourself. Don't. This is what is necessary to achieve great things. You have worked too hard to lose the edge now. You must remain in high gear.

As you prepare for exams, giving more attention to reviewing certain areas within a course is *not* the same as hoping parts of the course won't be tested, betting on that, and skipping the area altogether. I have seen students do this largely for two reasons: (1) they feel weak in a particular area and decide to ignore it and hope it won't be on their final exam, rather than tackling it until they have gained the requisite competence, or (2) a classmate or a student who had the professor in a previous semester says that area won't be tested. If it's in your book and on your syllabus, learn it. If the professor says it is within the scope of testable areas, learn it. Don't do the ostrich!

Confidence and strategy note: Try to separate what you know from what is confusing or uncertain for you. Your goal should be to have as much as possible in the "I know this" box, with as little as possible in the "I am not sure here" box. But keep these "boxes" separate! Don't let confusion about one or two points erode your confidence in what you do know. It is perfectly normal to be confused about certain rules. Think of learning in layers; keep adding new detail, new clarity, new depth of understanding without taking away any of the foundational layers you have built.

On actual exam days, employ the techniques we talked about in previous chapters on IRAC (or writing logically) and on how to approach exams. Also, think about the sleep, exercise, nutrition, meditation, and other self-care that will allow you to perform at peak levels.

Law school exams are a bit like Broadway shows or professional sporting events. (The bar exam is like the Super Bowl.) The more you can do to be prepared, in control, and feel good so that you can focus, the better.

Dress in layers. One day the school may crank up the air conditioning, another day it may feel like a furnace. Dressing in layers gives you a bit of control over your environment. Dress for success. For many of you, that may mean dressing as comfortably as possible—for example sweats, jeans, or leggings. Other people feel more powerful dressing in business attire, as if going to work. One former student said she wore a suit to all her finals; it made her feel like an attorney and she wrote her exams with more confidence than she would have wearing sweats. Whatever you wear, make sure you feel good and strong.

" 'Come to the edge,' He said. They said, 'We are afraid.' 'Come to the edge,' He said. They came. He pushed them ... and they flew."

—GUILLAUME APOLLINAIRE—

Final exams are your time to push off that edge and fly, to soar to success. It's OK to feel fear. But try to keep alongside those fears, the excitement and empowerment that come from rising to face challenges. When finals arrive you will be ready. Sure, it's scary. It's supposed to be. But tell yourself that you are ready. This is your moment.

> "Courage is resistance to fear, mastery
> of fear—not absence of fear."
>
> —MARK TWAIN—

Some things to remember when you go in to the exam room:

- Breathe.

You would be surprised how much better your brain functions when you just take deep breaths. Slow deep breathing will also help with test anxiety.

- Exams are puzzles.

If you love puzzles, think of the fact patterns as puzzles. Every fact is there on the paper for you; you just have to connect the dots. Let it be interesting!

- Exams are stories.

If you are more of a people person than a puzzle person, as you read exam questions, think of strolling through the ultimate cocktail party, where clusters of people tell you their stories and problems. In each situation, you have advice: good, solid, sound, and rationally reasoned answers!

Read exam questions as if they are real people's stories. In your mind are the rules that help unravel how each of those stories can play out. If they might well go one way or another, say that. ("Defendant will argue; plaintiff will argue; and the likely conclusion will be . . ."). Feel the incredible power that comes with knowing you can do that unraveling. You can and will pick apart each fact pattern and put it back together in a logical way that answers the questions asked.

- You worked hard and you are ready.

Take in and appreciate how hard you worked all semester. It's like being ready to run a marathon knowing that all your muscles are strong. The intellectual flab has melted away through the long hours of study and mental work-outs.

EXAMS

Appreciate how strong your wings are. When your first final exam approaches, push off despite the fears, with as much confidence as you can muster. You are ready.

PIF Reflection: Self-Care During Exam Days

1. What time is your first exam? What do you want to eat and what do you want/need to do before the test? What do you need with you? What will you read to warm up before your exam, so your mind is limber? How will you manage test anxiety? What is your plan?

2. What will you do after the first exam to rest and recharge? How will you re-charge? Who do you want to be around? Who do you want to avoid? When is your next exam? What can you do to best prepare for that one—mentally and physically?

3. What will you do after your last exam? Think about planning a trip or some special celebration. It may sound silly to celebrate because you won't have gotten grades yet, but this is not a celebration of how you did but that you did your best! It's not about the outcome but the process. It's a way to validate your own hard work and acknowledge the support of those who helped you along the way.

4. List two special things you can do within your budget for yourself and/or your family to acknowledge and celebrate that you made it through finals?

CHAPTER 14

SECOND SEMESTER, WORK ON IMPROVING FROM FIRST SEMESTER

When you have access to your grades, look carefully at them. (Feel free to read this chapter with a forward-looking eye if you have not yet received your first set of grades.)

Whatever your grades, it is important to remember that you are not your grades. I will talk about this below both in terms of those with top grades and those who will want to improve.

If your grades were excellent, you may want to skip this chapter, relax a bit, and re-focus on some other areas such as enhancing your self-care or expanding your circle by joining some student orgs or getting more active in student life. Do know, however, that some students with great grades first semester go in the opposite direction; rather than focusing beyond grades, they become even more fixated on retaining their GPAs. This can exacerbate stress. So, if this is you, try thinking back to your why (what brought you to law school), and try allowing yourself to feel passion for learning and to tap into your intellectual curiosity about every subject you are studying. Focus on study for learning sake and on taking care of yourself; success will follow.

Know too that what will make you a great lawyer involves building social skills and lawyering skills, along with content mastery. A worthwhile exercise to make this concrete is to review the 76 "foundations" that make up a "whole lawyer" in the map at: https://iaals.du.edu/projects/foundations-practice/foundations-maplearning and see how many of the foundations match qualities you possess. Look through the list and think of examples of experiences you have had that illustrate your competence/excellence in these. You may find this an empowering way to reinforce concretely that you are not your grades.

Given typical law school curves, many students will experience lower grades than they are used to. If any of your first grades were not as high as you wished, read on and make a plan to improve. And, try not to judge yourself or think any less of yourself as a person, student, or future lawyer. Try to think of grades as information to help design your personalized improvement plan.

An excellent first step—not easy for some students but often very helpful—is to talk with professors. Ask to review your final exam, not to change the grade but for feedback on how to improve. Welcome any input—even if it stings at first. For some, this is embarrassing or there is concern about disappointing a professor. But faculty want you to do well in the long run, and they understand that not everyone gets it all right away.

You can also make an appointment with your ASP faculty to discuss the exam process, your study habits, your confidence, and any strategies that might help you to do better the next semester.

Know that with every struggle, every so-called set back, you are learning lessons and developing resiliency. And, you will come out ahead if you go on and continue to make improvements.

Some may fear that you will lose job opportunities. If you are concerned, make an appointment with someone in your office of career services. They will help you strategize about employment in the most effective way for you.

One way to think about struggle is that it often makes you stronger. As you work to improve your academic performance in future semesters, ask yourself:

- What changes did I make to adapt to earlier struggles?"
- Did I figure out solutions to unanticipated changes or challenges?
- "What did I learn that would be useful to an employer?

Your answers might include specific examples of grit, resiliency, and positive or growth mindsets that helped you through these tough times. A record of clear improvement can provide powerful

SECOND SEMESTER, WORK ON IMPROVING FROM FIRST SEMESTER

evidence to future employers that you will demonstrate similar resilience as a professional, in other words, that you will fight for your clients as you did for yourself.

> **PIF Reflection for 1Ls in Their Second Semester**
>
> - What worked well for me and what didn't last semester?
>
> - What positive changes can I make this semester?
>
> - What can I do on my own and what help do I want/need from others?

"There are no secrets to success. It is the result of preparation, hard work, and learning from failure."

—COLIN POWELL—

While I love the quote above, I prefer the word "challenge" instead of "failure." For law school purposes, whatever causes challenges first semester or first year for that matter, the key is to see the struggle as a slight dip rather than a deep plunge, and persist.

Keep at it. Know that there is a grading curve in most law schools so only some small percentage of your class can get As. And, if you didn't get them this time, work to get them next semester, and the next, and the next. And, remember, all of your work during law school is a down payment for success on the bar exam and in practice. None of that effort is wasted.

Now I recognize that all of this positivity is easy to write and not always so easy to feel—especially if you are not in the A group, (often the top quartile depending on how your school ranks students). Quite likely you succeeded at most every academic opportunity prior to law school. You are used to getting As. Getting even a B can feel like a gut punch or kick in the teeth, especially for achievers.

But, you would not have gone to law school in the first place if you weren't a person who thrived on challenge. So even in the face of lower grades that might feel like setbacks, you must think of yourself *and speak of yourself* as someone who can *and will* succeed. Then, figure out what changes to make going forward. Instead of viewing a low grade as a setback, try to look at it as a set up for long-term success.

I feel like I should just give up!

While law school grades should not define you, many studies do show correlations with law school grade point averages (LGPA) and bar passage, so there are good reasons to learn from 1L exam experiences and make necessary adjustments *before you graduate and start studying for the bar exam.*

Tackle any concerns head-on. The longer you wait, the more you will suffer. Break through any pride, fear, shame, or whatever may be holding you back. Get on the path to success today. I assure you, you are not the only one with challenges. But you are the one who will most benefit if you seek and find effective help.

PIF Reflection:

- What would you tell a lawyer who lost a case?

- What will you do in law practice when you make mistakes?

- What steps do you take before you ask someone for help?

SECOND SEMESTER, WORK ON IMPROVING FROM FIRST SEMESTER

> • How do you feel when you ask someone for assistance?

If after your first semester, (or after midterms), your grades place you anywhere below where you would like to be, or if you find yourself struggling with academic, financial, psychological, or physical challenges in law school, you are not alone. You can find help and you can succeed. But you have to be willing to accept help and sometimes to affirmatively reach out. Asking for help is not easy. Many law students are concerned about seeming "stupid," "weak," or somehow "other" and not "belonging" by telling someone about struggles. They hope that challenges will just go away, that next semester will just be better, and that no one will have to know.

I get it. But know that you are much better served by action than wishful thinking. Remember, there is nothing wrong with *you*. It may just be that you need to *do* some things differently. And, small changes can make big differences.

- You might need to sleep more to focus better;
- You may need more exercise to relieve stress;
- You might need glasses or contact lenses, or to handle a medical problem that has been causing you pain;
- You might need to talk with a counselor, therapist, or someone from a local Lawyers Assistance Program (LAP);
- You might need some financial advice to get a handle on how you will repay your student loans or how you will budget the funds you currently have so that money worries don't keep you from studying;
- You might need a different, more conducive place to study;
- You might need techniques for listening more closely in class;

- You might need to review your notes right after each class and outline each week rather than waiting until the end of the semester;
- You might need to learn how to take notes that are helpful to you (or just take notes in the first place if you haven't been);
- You might need to complete practice exams and study sample answers, especially if you have professors who don't give midterms. (And, going forward, in classes where you *do* have midterms, you might benefit greatly from meeting with the professor to ask how you could have improved on your midterm exam.)
- And, you might need to dedicate more concentrated, focused time to active studying.

The key is to find what works for *you*. Once you know what to do, it may not be that difficult. I often tell students who are not quite where they want to be after first semester, "You are like a square peg trying to fit into a square hole; you are just tilted slightly diagonally. Make a few changes and you'll slide right in to where you need to be."

Know Your Strengths

Part of a dedicated improvement process is identifying weaker areas and strengthening them and building on already stronger areas. Consider the following:

Case briefing. Do you understand the reasoning in the cases you are reading? Are your reading and writing skills weaker than you would like them to be?

Note taking. Do you know how to take notes? Are your notes helpful to you? (Do you understand what you type? Can you read what you write?) Are you having a hard time concentrating?

Knowledge gaps. Are there areas within subjects you are taking that your professor did not cover or that you don't understand.

Skills. Do you need to improve your critical reading, effective writing, or typing speed and/or accuracy.

SECOND SEMESTER, WORK ON IMPROVING FROM FIRST SEMESTER

Physical health. Did you have a way of getting regular exercise? If not, start some sort of routine. Exercise consistently during school, while studying for the bar, and throughout your professional life. It helps relieve stress, increases your energy and acuity, and often makes you sleep better.

Get your eyes tested regularly and schedule a general physical exam if you have not had one recently. Tell your doctor if you have any concerns so that they can be addressed right away. (A student came to office hours toward the end of 3L describing back pain she feared might prevent her from sitting for three-hour blocks during the bar exam. She had suffered from this pain all through law school. How I wished she had sought help in 1L. I urged her to seek treatment immediately. Hopefully, that would help relieve the pain, but, if not, she needed to begin documenting the condition as soon as possible in case she needed accommodations during the bar exam.)

Mental health or substance use. These are critically important for law students and practicing lawyers; issues relating to either can not only affect your health, relationships, and academic success, but sometimes your moral character and fitness applications (part of the law licensing process). Get help if you need or want help. You are not alone. Talk with someone in Student Affairs, ASP, your law school (or main campus) counseling center, or consult your local lawyer assistance program (LAP). Boards of Law Examiners want you to get the help you need. Not getting help will likely impact you far more negatively.

Again if you are avoiding help because you are concerned that your bar license application process may be adversely impacted, make an appointment with your Dean of Students or a Lawyers Assistance Program (LAP) in your jurisdiction.

"Lawyer Assistance Programs provide confidential services and support to judges, lawyers and law students who are facing substance use disorders or mental health issues. If you or someone you know is in need of assistance, contact your state or local LAP." (This language comes from the ABA's comprehensive state-by-state directory of LAPs at https://www.americanbar.org/groups/lawyer_assistance/resources/lap_programs_by_state/). Help from LAPs is confidential and can assist in planning ahead and working through any potential moral character or fitness issues. You will also find useful information in this free online pamphlet, also on the ABA website, *Substance Abuse & Mental Health Toolkit, for Law School Students and Those Who Care About Them.*

Assess How Far off You Were

If you were close to being on target with grades, you may simply need some fine-tuning or minor adjustments.

Obtain practice tests or released exams with sample passing answers, and study them. Start by trying to find your own professors' past exams. Many law libraries and ASP faculty keep them and will give you copies if you simply ask. Professors often will do this, too. (Students frequently share that their grades significantly increased after they have found the courage to talk to their professors and ask them for help.)

If you are further off the mark—for instance, if you are in the bottom quarter of your class, find out why and get help now. Use your school's resources, starting with ASP faculty, student affairs office, law librarian, and/or a professor with whom you feel comfortable. Beware of commercial entities preying on law students' fears and trying to sell you solutions. There are no quick fixes. You need to figure out for yourself or with the help of a reliable resource (be that a person, book, or video) what you need to adjust. Are you not devoting enough time to your studies? Are you genuinely not getting it? Have you tried hornbooks to help pull the material together? Do you read passages twice or three times? Do whatever it takes. Seek reliable feedback to learn where you are and why, make a turnaround/improvement plan, and get back on track as soon as possible.

Changing Habits

Part of your improvement process is adding or changing habits—this can include taking practice tests, studying in a different location, seeking help, making more time for study generally, and taking any number of different steps. But doing the exact same thing and hoping for change is not likely to work. Below are some ideas on changes that have helped many of my former students.

SECOND SEMESTER, WORK ON IMPROVING FROM FIRST SEMESTER

Incorporate practice exams into your study schedule. Practice tests are like exercise: continuing the habit is easier than starting it. Let's say you are taking Constitutional Law. Well in advance of the final, locate copies of any released exams your professor has on file. Ask your professor if you cannot find these on your own. (If your professor will not release past exams, talk with your ASP faculty and/or law librarian to locate other reputable sources for old exams.) Next, while the material is fresh (either just before or just after the final exam), take a look at some past bar exam questions in Constitutional Law (essays or MCQs).

Seek help. Reliable help can come from books, online resources, or from someone smart and supportive. It may be a faculty member, recent graduate, or another student who is in 2L or 3L. For book recommendations, consult your law librarian and/or ASP faculty and the websites of reputable publishers.

Make More Time for Study: Choose Your Analogy

Sometimes, it's hard to wrap our heads around why law school reading and studying takes so long. It may feel like something is wrong with you when you are putting in so many hours and still not feeling like it's sufficient. Or, you may admit to yourself that you really just didn't put in enough time first semester.

Let's look at a few analogous areas in life so you remind yourself how normal it is to have to put in a lot of time. Glance through these five examples and pick the one that works for you: fitness, finance, sports or arts, cooking, or event planning. You only need one.

Fitness Analogy

Many of us wish there were a way to waive a magic wand and become the fit person we hope to be. But diet pills have side effects. And crash dieting and crash exercise programs usually do not achieve sustained fitness. Most fitness experts counsel incremental approaches. Slow and steady. They are not particularly fun. Not exciting or dramatic. But these steps (pun intended), especially when taken together, often lead to healthier paths—drink more water, take the stairs instead of the elevator, move/exercise, eat smaller portions, eat fewer carbs, limit alcohol, reduce sugar intake, etc.

Studying to do well in law school is similar to a long-term fitness routine; a steady progression of gaining familiarity and fluency with subject areas, and then a commitment to regular and intense training and practice that will result in the skills necessary to succeed on law school exams.

None of these happen overnight. Anyone selling programs, courses, or systems to make it "easy" is selling bogus diet pills. On the other hand, the process of studying does not need to be painful; if someone says that you must suffer tremendously, well, that's their story. It doesn't have to be yours. Daily study and exam training are hard habits to launch, but just like taking the stairs instead of the elevator (not comfortable the first few times), you get acclimated. And, eventually, it starts to feel good. As your muscles get stronger—as your critical reading, content mastery, and test-taking skills improve, you start feeling your power and enjoying the process. Indeed, the whole thing becomes a positive, virtuous cycle.

Sometimes, we can use tools to springboard into certain actions—for example, step counting technology has led many to "compete" with themselves, family, or friends to boost activity. Certain experts suggest using smaller plates to "trick" one's mind into thinking a portion is the same when it's smaller. These tools facilitate taking the incremental steps; they are not solutions in and of themselves. The same is true with studying. There are tools to help you increase the time and efficacy of your learning.

PIF Reflection: Jumpstart Your Studying

1. List three things that get you cranking, for example a study app where you track hours or study group (like a book club where you feel guilty if you don't read the book):

2. Does your studying improve and do you feel better about it when you sleep sufficiently, eat healthy foods, and exercise? (And, if you think you don't have time to do those things, think again. You may find the

SECOND SEMESTER, WORK ON IMPROVING FROM FIRST SEMESTER 153

> time savings when you are healthy in mind and body far outweigh the extra forced and unproductive hours.)

Personal Finance Analogy

It might help to think of your 1L grades as similar to money, and your GPA as your financial portfolio. In blunt terms, if you are in the red, below where you need to be, in "deficit spending" mode, figure out what you need to do to slowly and steadily bring your law school "balance sheet" from the red into the black—from deficit into breaking even, and then, by graduation, into a surplus that will help you to pass that bar exam first time around.

And, what happens if you continue in the red? Bill collectors and possibly bankruptcy—or law school equivalents probation or dismissal. If it strings out long enough, you might graduate but not pass the bar, putting you in long-term deficit mode.

How does one bring finances into balance? Budget. Earn more and/or spend less. Save wherever you can. How does this fit into studying? Same way. You need to "budget," considering both the quantity and quality of your study habits. Increase your focus, augment the hours you put in, reduce distractions, and enhance your study strategies. Engaging and struggling with both the big picture (how a topic or sub-topic fits within a subject) and the details (rules and exceptions to those rules), and completing practice tests and studying sample answers all help much more than endless re-reading or highlighting.

So, look at your current schedule, including all your law school and non-law school commitments, and your current study habits, and come up with some steps you can take beginning today to get on and stay on a path to improvement.

Athletics or Arts Analogy

Have you ever thought about how many hours it takes athletes to gain the skills they have when you watch them compete in the big game or the Olympics, or the work it has taken behind the scenes when you see or hear your favorite artist at a concert or on Broadway?

Malcom Gladwell in <u>Outliers</u> explains that "mastery" is achieved when someone "practices a skill, such as playing the violin" for 10,000 hours. Do the math; between law school and bar preparation you should be at about that amount of time before you are licensed. Review the earlier chapter on protecting and managing your time. Look at your typical week now and at how much time you devote to law school and what else takes the rest of your time. Figure out how to reduce the time claimed by everything that takes you away your studies.

Now, I am not saying that it's only a matter of hours. There are people who sit diligently for hours on end, highlighting in various colors, skimming material, reviewing and reviewing but never really understanding or "owning" what they think they are "learning." Quality is of course essential. But quantity counts as well, and deep learning often takes more time than you think it will. So, look at your schedule and see how much time you are now putting in and plot a path that increases your focused study hours (without decreasing your sleep or exercise time). That alone may improve your potential for excellence in law school (and first-time bar passage after you graduate).

<u>Cooking Analogy</u>

Do you like to cook—or do you like cooking shows? Just like athletes and artists, chefs train for years before preparing consistently delicious and beautifully presented dishes. The first months of culinary school are notorious for including repetitive training for many hours in knife skills. It looks easy when you see people cut onions in a uniform dice, but that ease results from many hours of labor. (And, probably many tears. Cutting onions, right?) Knife skills don't come from watching videos and reading books about the process; one must actually practice wielding sharp knives, over and over again. Think of yourself in the months of law school as that would be chef picking up the knife for the first time. Eventually, you'll be a pro, but it won't happen overnight.

SECOND SEMESTER, WORK ON IMPROVING FROM FIRST SEMESTER

Event Planning Analogy

Some events can be planned in weeks, or days. But elaborate weddings or large-scale conferences often take months or years to plan. Typical wedding planning articles list action items for at least 12 months before the event. You must pick a date (considering time of year, other obligations, who you want to attend, etc.), create a budget, choose a venue, decide who will be in the wedding and secure their commitments, determine what food will be served (and how to handle dietary restrictions), what sort of ceremony will you have, who will officiate, how many guests, any limits of types of guests, choose flowers, choose and purchase what the couple will wear and what others in the wedding party wear, plan any other events around the wedding (bachelor/bachelorette party, rehearsal dinner), handle any legal implications of the event (change of name, change of status for taxes, insurance), etc. Law school finals (and the bar exam after you graduate) are also big events that must be planned for. How can you start planning now to improve on your next set of exams?

PIF Reflection: Planning Ahead

Describe an event you planned a long time for?

What sorts of steps did you take?

What was the outcome?

What would you do differently if you were planning it again?

> What lessons could you take away to help you plan for success on future law school exams?

Think Carefully About Courses You Select in 2L and 3L

Most 1Ls do not get many choices in terms of course selection. But you will likely have many options in upper division years. Consider taking classes in areas you think you might want to practice in—and in areas you have absolutely no plan to work in but are fascinated with. Take classes with professors who are reputed to be excellent. And, consider taking all or most bar subjects offered, even if they aren't required courses. Here I say *consider* because studies don't indicate a strong correlation between having taken all or most bar courses and bar passage. You may learn more and develop stronger legal analysis, reasoning, and writing skills by taking an elective course that you are "into" than by taking another bar course. I am certain that the many clinical courses I took in law school were instrumental in my having passed the bar exam the first time. These courses focused not only on legal analysis but on factual analysis in a way that proved critical for bar success.

It's also true that some course selections are best not because of content but because of a particular professor. It can be transformative to study with someone who inspires you or with a leading scholar in a particular field. One of my favorite classes, and the one that inspired me to teach law, was Street Law. It was also taught by one of my favorite professors.

So, since I've noted good reasons to take courses other than bar courses and acknowledged that there may not be a strong correlation between law school curriculum and bar passage, why am I suggesting that some students may be well served by taking as many bar subjects as possible during school? Because bar review can be far less stressful when students are reviewing material, rather than learning it for the first time. Some people are downright freaked out when they realize how much brand-new material they must master. So, especially if 1L was a struggle, my suggestion here to *consider* taking bar courses is

SECOND SEMESTER, WORK ON IMPROVING FROM FIRST SEMESTER

about your *comfort level* with having to quickly learn so much new material after graduation not your *ability* to learn what you need. You likely can learn a whole lot without having taking the courses during law school. But, skipping such courses may cause yourself needless anxiety. If you decide for good reasons not to take certain classes during school, make time to study those subjects at least briefly before graduation—so they are not brand new during bar review. For example, during winter or spring break in 3L, get a reliable hornbook, study guide, or audio or video lecture that gives an overview of the subjects. (More on bar prep in my book, Bar Exam Success: A Comprehensive Guide.)

CHAPTER 15

DRAFT YOUR LAW SCHOOL SUCCESS PLAN

We have covered a lot of what will surface in 1L, so this is a good time to pull it together and begin drafting a law school success plan—a living document that you'll continue updating throughout law school and eventually morph into a bar success plan for the months after graduation.

What goes into such a plan? Everything we've talked about so far in this workbook! Study habits, outlining, taking practice tests, protecting your time, physical and mental health needs, self-care, confidence, and more.

Your plan should include something on your law school finances. Money is a difficult subject for many people to talk about, but the people in your financial aid office are there for you. Meet with them and discuss not just funding for each semester but make sure you understand what costs will be hitting when down the road and have a plan to save for those. There are many expenses beyond tuition, books, and living expenses—both during law school and immediately after you graduate when you will study preferably full-time for the bar exam. But the answer to *money* issues cannot be to just work, or work more, because you need *time* for study, self-care, and building relationships—both during and after law school.

A useful free resource for law students is the online program MAX by AccessLex. This helps give you the financial literacy to manage your own money and get a head start on what you will need to learn as a lawyer when you may well be responsible for other people's money.

Time may be easier to talk about than money, but not easier to make. Everything takes longer than you think it will, so you must work actively to free up time for both studying during the semester and extra time to study for finals. Re-read the earlier chapters on distractions and protecting your time. Plan ahead if you need to line up care for children, elderly relatives, and pets, and/or take off time from work to prepare for and take exams. These can be hard to arrange at the last minute and much easier with a lot of lead time. Especially if you are working, try to take vacation time or unpaid leave to study for finals. If you get involved in student orgs, think about and plan for reducing your volunteer hours before midterms and finals.

One thing that both takes time and makes time is exercise. If you do not have a daily exercise routine, start one. You will need this stress release during finals, and it will help you to focus better now. I am *not* suggesting you try a new sport or do anything strenuous that you are not used to. But if you are not currently very active, you will be surprised by how much better you will feel and better you handle stress by adding even a daily walk into your routine. The added focus when you study and ability to sleep better will more than make up for the time you spend exercising.

Bottom line, ideally you want your plan to include at least something on the following:

- Study (think of this as your full-time job as a law student)
- Physical and Mental Wellness
- Creative Outlets
- Spiritual/Faith/Meditation Practice
- Relationships (family, friends, partner if you have one)
- Finances

And, as we said, you want to treat your success plan as a living document that you update regularly, at least each semester and when circumstances change. One thing you may add in second semester of 1L or in 2L for sure is some sort of service. Whether it's service to the law school or the community, doing something to help others is not only intrinsically good but it can often help with your own work-life balance.

DRAFT YOUR LAW SCHOOL SUCCESS PLAN

> *"Before everything else, getting ready is the secret of success."*
>
> —HENRY FORD—

OK, you can start with the template below and add or modify sections as you need or want. Remember, you can show someone else your plan or you can keep it as something that is just for you.

1L Success Plan

The following are points I will keep in mind as I work through the semester, thinking both backward from final exams to now, and forward from now through the end of exams. And, I will update this plan regularly.

√ **My main goals are:**

_____.

√ **Finals**

Finals weeks are:
The dates/times of each of my exams are:
I have let people in my world know that I will be "gone" during finals time.
[ ] Yes [ ] Not yet but I will do this by _____.

Dedicated Time

I have dedicated _____ hours per week for study throughout the semester, and I plan to re-assess that each month to make sure that I have carved out enough time.

I will increase the number of hours I regularly study to _____ hours per week the month before finals to be in "high gear."

For working students: I have made a schedule so that I can study on top of my work during the semester, and I have requested time off to focus on finals. [ ] Yes [ ] No

(To do by the month before finals) I have cleared my calendar during finals of any commitments (professional, social, or otherwise) that I can put off until after finals, including: _____

√ **Relationships**

I may have less time, but I spend at least some regular, quality time with friends, family, and/or my partner/spouse. [ ] Yes [ ] No

I have worked to make sure that the people in my life know how to best support me in my law school journey. [ ] Yes [ ] Not yet, but working on it

_____
_____

√ **Managing Distractions & Protecting Time**

I have identified the following as potentially taking time away from my studies, (e.g., friends and family members who text me all the time):

_____
_____

My biggest distractions tend to be (e.g., binge-watching; once I get into a series, I can't stop):

_____
_____

I will eliminate/reduce the following distractions and defer the following obligations until after finals:

> Example 1: The month before finals I will deactivate my social media accounts and reactivate them after exams.

> Example 2: I will put my phone in the other room while I study, and look at it only at times when I am ready to take a break.

_____
_____

√ **Law School Budget**

Estimated total of funds needed this semester: $_____

Estimated total of funds on hand: $_____

If there is a shortfall, I have a plan to make up the difference either by reducing my spending or increasing my funding [ ] Yes [ ] Not yet.

DRAFT YOUR LAW SCHOOL SUCCESS PLAN 163

_____ (perhaps in the financial aid office) is someone with whom I can reliably discuss financial questions.

I have read books on or taken a course on law school finances, such as the free online MAX by AccessLex, and I understand my student loan obligations [ ] Yes [ ] Not yet

√ Written Study Schedule

I have a written study schedule [ ] Yes [ ] Not yet and I will create a written study schedule by _____.

The following are places I can study effectively, without interruption (e.g., office, home, law library) _____.

People in my inner circle know my study schedule so they know when I cannot be interrupted. [ ] Yes [ ] Not yet

My study schedule includes hours for specific tasks, such as:

- Reading and case briefing _____
- Learning legal rules and concepts _____
- Creating my own outlines _____
- Taking practice exams _____

√ Calendaring System

[ ] I calendar all deadlines, commitments, appointments, etc. in my phone laptop, tablet, or planner

[ ] I have an effective reminder system.

√ Confidence and Motivation

At this point, my greatest strengths are:

1. _____
2. _____
3. _____

At this point, my biggest challenges are:

1. _____
2. _____
3. _____

√ Health and Wellness

Health issues:

I have taken steps to deal with any health issues that might interfere with my ability to do my best in school. [ ] Yes [ ] No

I think I need accommodations and have talked with the Dean of Students. [ ] Yes [ ] No

I am on top of routine preventive medical care, including I have had my vision and hearing checked in the past year. [ ] Yes [ ] No

I have taken steps to arrange for any needed care for children, or other dependent care: [ ] Yes [ ] No

I regularly do _____ for exercise.

I prioritize getting sufficient sleep. [ ] Yes [ ] Not yet, but working on it.

√ Creative Outlets

To relieve stress and maintain balance, I do something regularly that is creative or silly—that is not for a "score" or "grade," somewhere where it does not matter how "good" I am at it. [ ] Yes [ ] No, [ ] Not yet.

I make time for fun: [ ] Yes [ ] No, [ ] Not yet.

√ Service

I do _____ to be of service to others.

√ Spiritual/Faith/Meditation Practice

I have some spiritual, religious, relaxation, or other non-law related activity as a regular practice. [ ] Yes [ ] No, [ ] Not yet.

I make time for the following: _____

√ Other Areas I Know I Must Plan For in Order to Be Successful in Law School

1.
2.
3.

UPDATING MY SUCCESS PLAN

I will make time to review, edit, and update this plan regularly and at a minimum each semester. [ ] Yes

END OF WORKING DRAFT SUCCESS PLAN

CHAPTER 16

THINKING AHEAD TO AFTER 1L

Many 1Ls spend time and energy securing jobs for the summer after 1L. The most important thing with respect to jobs is listening to your law school career services center. They will help you write and/or edit your resume and cover letter, and find places to apply for summer jobs. They can't guarantee you a position, but their help is invaluable, if you listen.

Some Interviewing Strategies

Again, your career services office will have specific advice for in-person or video interviews. The list below represents just a few points to keep in mind, after you get your foot in the door for an interview. Again, when in doubt, follow the advice given by your law school's Office of Career Services.

- Make the best impression possible, but be yourself.
- Make sure your clothes are clean. Note: Dress even for a video interview; too many people are caught by surprise if the camera inadvertently moves or if the interviewer asks you to stand up!
- Arrive on time (better still, arrive early).
- Bring an extra résumé with you. Bring a writing sample and list of references, if appropriate. Put those documents in a portfolio or binder in which you also include some blank paper if there is anything you want to note. (Be sure you have sent any requested documents before any video or phone interviews.)
- Study up ahead of time on the people who will interview you. Research the individuals and study the law firm, company, or organization. Determine its philosophy. Research cases on which individuals have worked. Read their publications. Get their

- résumés. Find out where they went to school. Note any points you may have in common with them.

- Develop two lists of questions: (1) what the interviewers may ask you and (2) what you will ask them! Prepare your responses to what they will likely ask you. (Why do you want the job? How do you stand out? Why will you be successful? How will you help their office, practice, company?) Anticipate questions and develop confident, appropriate answers about holes in your résumé or other potential weaknesses. Next, try to list at least two things you want to know about them (that you couldn't find out by looking at online resources). Asking questions is important—it shows your enthusiasm, curiosity, and intelligence. Pay close attention to the answers, so you can follow up, too.

- Send a thank you note after the interview! This is the easiest advice and something fewer and fewer people do. But writing thank you notes is essential to your future networking, whether or not you get any particular job.

Find a Career Mentor

A career mentor may be the same person as your law school mentor, but it can be someone different. The person may help you strategize about finding job opportunities or whether to take a job if you receive multiple offers. Meeting with your career mentors during your summer at least once may also help you to assess if this is a job you might be interested in after law school, and how to get the most out of the summer experience.

Transferable Skills

To prove to yourself that you can perform well, think of skills and qualities of an effective lawyer. (One place to look for this is at the website of the Denver-based nonprofit, the Institute for the Advancement of the American Legal System (IAALS, see https://iaals.du.edu/projects/foundations-practice/foundations-

THINKING AHEAD TO AFTER 1L 167

map.) Take either the five broad categories (communicator, practitioner, professional, problem solver, self-starter), or the 76 distinct foundations from this IAALS study, and list specific experiences that demonstrate you possess these skills. Consider what you have done in and outside of school, including before law school, with work, family, community, professional, or political organizations to which you belong to or for which you volunteer. Think also about hobbies you pursue.

In the spaces below, write examples of experiences that demonstrate your skills. Be as specific as possible. This is just for your own brainstorming. You may translate this into a cover letter and perhaps into talking points for an interview, or it may just improve your own self-confidence and awareness that the person you are and the professional you are becoming will be a great lawyer.

PIF Exercise: My Transferable Skills

I have good research skills. What shows this is:

_____

I communicate well. To demonstrate this, consider:

_____

I reason well as is evidenced by:

_____

I am organized and responsible. Proof of this is:

_____

I am technologically competent (savvy). My work with the following demonstrates my skills:

_____

I am an effective problem-solver. Experiences that point to this are:

I consider myself a self-starter as evidenced by my:

List some other skills that would be of value to an employer and evidence of your possessing those skills:

Conclusion

This workbook is about *success*—in law school and in life. Success means different things to different people. All good. You want to live your best life not anyone else's.

Throughout this workbook, we have focused on some common denominators.

- Success is not about unattainable dreams, fantasies, or quick fixes. Nowhere did we say, "Just be confident and all will be well."

- There are no magic wands. Law school is a bit like a gym. Getting in is like getting a membership. But you must do more than simply sign up and pay the fee to get fit. Similarly, getting accepted and paying tuition bills will not get you through law school.

- Beware of anyone who promises quick and easy paths to success. Good teachers (be they professors or classmates) can clarify confusion and simplify complex concepts, but they can't and shouldn't try to make law school easy.

- You may need to ask for additional help –and that is perfectly fine and entirely normal. The best place to start is free: your law library! Many of the reliable publishers have subscription services and your law school purchases that content for you; all you have to do is log in with your law school email and create an account. You may want to buy some supplemental materials, but check with the law library first.

Remember the success strategies outlined in this workbook and your own reflections about yourself as a student and future professional.

I hope this workbook has helped you to view law school as equally challenging and rewarding—not easy but wholly doable, and worth all the effort. Your legal education is a power tool for social change. Wield it well.

Carry a positive mindset with you on your journey. And, let power and positivity accompany you with each step forward.

Dive in. Embrace the struggles. You will prevail. With what you learn, and your law degree and license, you will have the potential to do well and do good—for life!

PIF Reflection:

What does becoming a lawyer mean to you?

_____
_____
_____

What changes have you noticed in yourself since you started law school?

_____
_____
_____

What do you see changing in your life once you have your law license?

_____
_____
_____

What are you thinking about now that you want to remind yourself of next year? Five years from now?

_____
_____
_____

GLOSSARY OF LAW SCHOOL TERMS

Below are simple definitions of some common law school terms. What other new words have you learned in 1L so far that are not on this list? Are there terms you've heard that you do not understand? Read through the list below and try to use each term in a sentence. Terminology mastery paves the way success in your first year and beyond.

Definitions marked with an asterisk are reproduced from The Criminal Law Handbook: Know Your Rights, Survive the System and Represent Yourself in Court: How to Prepare and Try a Winning Case, both published by nolo.com and co-authored by Sara Berman and Paul Bergman. Many law students find reading these books provide a clear and empowering overview of the civil and criminal justice systems respectively.

ABA: American Bar Association. Professional association of lawyers; body that accredits law schools. The ABA has a law student division, https://abaforlawstudents.com/ and publishes many books and magazines including the *Student Lawyer*.

*Acquit: A judge or jury "acquits" a defendant by finding the defendant not guilty.

*Acquittal: A final judgment that a defendant is not guilty.

*Administrative agency: A government department charged with enforcing laws and developing regulations. For example, the Department of Homeland Security is a federal agency that enforces laws relating to public safety, and it has the power to develop regulations.

*Admissible evidence: Evidence that a trial judge can consider or can allow a jury to consider when reaching a verdict.

Affinity groups: Student groups that have common interests.

Affirm: Action a court takes to uphold a judgment of a lower court.

*Affirmative defense: A type of defense that a defendant has to assert and support with evidence, such as self-defense.

*Appeal: A request to a higher court to review the rulings or decision of a trial court judge. Appeals are often heard by panels of three judges, who do not reweigh the evidence but rather focus on claimed legal errors.

*Appellant: The party who appeals to an appellate court.

*Appellate court: A higher court that reviews the decision of a lower court.

*Appellee: Party who responds to an appeal brought by an appellant.

*Argument: A rhetorical presentation that supports or refutes legal claims—this term is used both in law school exams and in litigation (see IRAC below)

*Attorney: Another name for a lawyer. Also called "counselor."

Bar: Several meanings: 1) short for bar exam, 2) a word to describe a community of practicing lawyers, or 3) partition separating spectators from attorneys and judge in a courtroom.

Bar exam: High stakes exam required in nearly every state in order to become a licensed lawyer. See UBE below.

Bar preparation: general term for months of intensive review and study needed to pass the bar exam.

Bar review: courses designed to review the law and provide practice exam opportunities to get ready to pass the bar exam.

*Beyond a reasonable doubt: The burden of proof that the prosecution must carry in a criminal trial to obtain a guilty verdict.

Blackboard: Learning management system used for course syllabi, assessments, and other resources.

Black's Law Dictionary: A comprehensive dictionary of legal terms used by many law students and lawyers.

Bluebook: Guide to uniform citations used in legal documents and publications.

*Brief: A written argument submitted to support a party's legal position, often prepared as part of an appeal. Also used as a verb, "to brief cases" meaning to summarize key components of an appellate opinion. (See case brief below.)

GLOSSARY OF LAW SCHOOL TERMS 173

CALI: Nonprofit organization, the Center for Computer-Assisted Legal Instruction that hosts online lessons and tutorials to help law students is often shortened as CALI (pronounced "kal-ee"). The CALI website is https://cali.org/.

Canvas: Learning management system used for course syllabi, assessments, and other resources.

Case: Legal claim that parties bring to court; also, a court decision

Casebook: Course text assigned in most law school courses comprised primarily of edited appellate court cases.

Case brief: As you read cases for class, you will want to "brief" them. You will receive instruction on how to do this, likely during orientation. Essentially, it is a summary of the case, so that you can remember things like important facts, issues, and the holding, when you are called on in class, and when you need to study and review. At a minimum, your case briefs should include the title of the case (and page number in your casebook), the key facts, the issue(s), the holding(s), the court's rationale, dissenting opinions.

*Case citation: Information for locating an appellate court opinion. Example: The citation of Miranda v. Arizona, 384 U.S. 436 (1966), indicates that the Supreme Court opinion begins on page 436 of Volume 384 of United States Reports.

Case law: Law based on cases or judicial opinions rather than law based on statutes, or other written laws.

*Certiorari: A petition for certiorari asks a higher court to exercise discretion and review a lower court's ruling

Citation: (See case citation.)

Civil: Noncriminal. Civil lawsuits are typically between private parties—compared with criminal cases that involve government enforcement of criminal laws. A situation may involve both a criminal prosecution and a civil action.

Civility: habits of courtesy and politeness that lawyers and law students are expected to maintain as professionals.

Civ Pro: An abbreviation for Civil Procedure, a law school course that deals with rules regarding the process of bringing and litigating civil matters.

Clerk/clerking: Assistants to judges who work in courts to help judges conduct research and write judicial decisions. Note: there is also a clerk of court, in addition to individual judge's clerks.

Law graduates may clerk for a judge after graduation. Talk with your Career counselor to learn more about clerking opportunities.

Clinic: Law school law office and training program where law students represent clients and work on real cases.

Cold Call: Expression used when a law professor asks a particular student to discuss cases assigned as reading or answer some other questions, without giving the student advanced warning.

Commercial outline: see outline.

***Common law:** Laws that originate in judicial opinions rather than legislatures.

Conclusory: Term often used to critique of legal writing that suggests a conclusion was reached without sufficient factual and/or legal analysis.

Con Law: Abbreviation for Constitutional Law.

Crim or Crim Law: Abbreviation for Criminal Law.

Crim Pro: Abbreviation for Criminal Procedure (something called constitutional criminal procedure).

Defendant: The party tried for a crime in criminal case; the party sued in a civil case. May be abbreviated with the Greek letter Delta that looks like a triangle (Δ).

***Dicta:** Language in appellate court decisions that indicates judges' attitudes but is unnecessary to case outcomes. One of my favorite law professors (UCLA Professor Emeritus Paul Bergman) refers to this as judges' "Oh, by the way" comments.

***Dissenting opinion:** An appellate court judge's written reasons for disagreeing with the outcome of a case. Judges may prepare dissenting opinions in the hope of influencing judges in

GLOSSARY OF LAW SCHOOL TERMS 175

higher courts or in future cases, or to encourage legislators to change laws.

Elements: Component parts of a legal rule, all of which must be proven. (Compare with factors).

*Evidence: Course in law school that covers rules regarding and also the name for information presented to a judge or jury, including the testimony of witnesses, documents, and exhibits.

*Fifth Amendment right against self-incrimination: The constitutional right of every person to remain silent when being questioned by the police and—as a criminal defendant—to decline to testify.

FRCP: Federal Rules of Civil Procedure.

*Holding: A rule of law established by an appellate court opinion.

Hornbook: Text that explains areas of law in prose, similar to a college textbook.

Hypo: (abbreviation for hypothetical). Fictional factual scenario.

IRAC: Abbreviation for Issue, Rule, Analysis, Conclusion, a logical format for legal writing often preferred on exams.

JD: Juris doctor

*Jurisdiction: Term that means a court's power and legal authority to hear a case (for example, "Nevada courts had jurisdiction to try a resident of Montana who was charged with committing a crime in Nevada."); also, a term describing a territory within which a particular legal system operates (For example, more than 35 jurisdictions currently use the UBE as their bar exam.)

K: Abbreviation for contract and for $1,000.

Law journals: Student run publications, often topical such as the Journal of Race, Gender & Ethnicity.

Law review: Student run legal publications. You may have an opportunity to join one your second year, which means you will be editing the articles that the publications put out. The articles are typically written by law professors around the country.

Lexis/Westlaw: Legal resource databases. You will get logins to use these and learn to use them in Legal Process courses.

LSAC: Law School Admission Council, https://www.lsac.org/.

MBE: Multistate bar exam, the multiple-choice portion of the NY bar exam, see https://www.ncbex.org/exams/mbe/.

MEE: Multistate essay exam, the essay part of the NY bar exam see https://www.ncbex.org/exams/mee/.

Mental health toolkit: document published by the ABA that includes mental health and substance use information and resources for law students https://www.americanbar.org/content/dam/aba/administrative/lawyer_assistance/ls_colap_mental_health_toolkit_new.pdf.

Moot court: Simulated courtroom experience for law students.

MPRE: Multistate professional responsibility exam, a separate exam testing legal ethics that you have to take, in addition to the bar exam. See https://www.ncbex.org/exams/mpre/.

MPT: Multistate performance test, see https://www.ncbex.org/exams/mpt/.

NCBE: National Conference of Bar Examiners, national nonprofit that administers the UBE and other aspects of attorney licensure, see https://www.ncbex.org.

NYLC: The New York Law Course, which is a course required to take before the NYLE and in order to be licensed to practice law in NY, see https://www.nybarexam.org/Content/Course Materials.htm.

NYLE: The New York Law Exam, required along with other exams and requirements, to be licensed to practice law in NY, see https://www.nybarexam.org/Content/CourseMaterials.htm.

One L: Also, 1L. Term meaning first year law students. Each subsequent year is called 2L, 3L, (and 4L for part-time students) respectively. This is also the title of a novel written by author Scott Turow about his experiences as a first-year law student at Harvard Law.

*Opinions: Appellate court judges' written explanations for their decisions. These are what you read in your casebooks

GLOSSARY OF LAW SCHOOL TERMS 177

Outline: Noun meaning a summary of a law course. Verb meaning to summarize a course. Students should outline all your courses using all sorts of study strategies that help to engage with and understand the material including but not limited to writing concepts in your own words, making graphs and flow charts, drawing pictures, making audio or video recordings. When publishers sell these, they are often called "commercial outlines." While consulting a commercial outline may be helpful, it is important to make your own outlines so that you gain a deep and full understanding of all your courses.

*Parties: Adversaries in court. The government and defendants are the parties to a criminal case.

*Petitioner: A party who makes a formal written request to a higher court asking it to review the ruling of a lower court.

Plaintiff: Party bringing a civil lawsuit, often abbreviated with a Greek letter Pi.

Prosecutor: Government lawyer bringing and litigating criminal case.

PSLF: Public Service Loan Forgiveness, see https://studentaid.gov/manage-loans/forgiveness-cancellation/public-service.

Respondent: In an appeal, the party seeking to uphold a decision by a lower court.

Reverse: Verb used when a higher court overrules a decision of a lower court.

SBA: Student Bar Association

SCOTUS: Supreme Court of the United States, learn more at https://www.supremecourt.gov/.

Statutory law: Law based on statutes as opposed to case law (see above).

Student orgs: Student Organizations.

Supplements: Term used to describe law school study aids law. Some of these are more reliable than others. Check with your professors, law librarians, and ASP faculty if you have questions about particular supplements.

Torts: Civil wrongs for which people generally may seek money. Many acts, such as assault and battery, are both crimes and torts. Torts and criminal law are both required first year subjects.

TWEN: Legal education course management system that was frequently used before learning management systems such as Blackboard and Canvas.

UBE: Uniform Bar Exam. https://www.ncbex.org/exams/ube/. Many states including New York use the UBE as their bar exam. Other states such as Florida and California administer their own exam. UBE scores may be portable or transferable between UBE states.

UCC: Uniform Commercial Code, laws that govern commercial transactions. You may study parts of this Code in your contracts course and in other courses.

Additional Legal Terms

Below are terms not defined in the Glossary above that you will want to become fluent with as you progress in your law studies. Some of these you will learn and use in specific classes; others may be part of the general language of lawyering. Look them up in your legal dictionary and write your own definitions.

Affidavit:

Arraignment:

Arrest:

Assault:

Attempt:

Attorney work product:

Authenticate:

Bail:

Bailiff:

Battery:

Best evidence rule:

Bill of Rights:

GLOSSARY OF LAW SCHOOL TERMS 179

Booking:

Burglary:

Business records exception:

Capital crime:

Challenge:

Challenge for cause:

Chambers (also called judge's chambers):

Charge(s):

Circumstantial evidence:

Clear and convincing evidence:

Closing argument:

Complaint:

Conspiracy:

Contempt of Court:

Cross examination:

Direct examination:

Discovery:

Double jeopardy:

Due process:

Ex parte:

Ex post facto:

Excited utterance:

Exclusionary rule:

Exhibit:

Expert witness:

Felony:

Foundation:

Frivolous motion:

Fruit of the poisonous tree:

Grand jury:
Habeas corpus:
Hearing:
Hearsay:
Impeach:
Inadmissible:
Incompetence to stand trial:
Indictment:
Indigent:
Information:
Infraction:
Insanity:
Irrelevant:
Jail:
Judge:
Juror:
Jury:
Juvenile:
Juvenile court:
Larceny:
Leading question:
Lesser-included offense:
Lineup:
Magistrate:
Malice:
Manslaughter:
Mens rea:
Miranda warning:
Misdemeanors:

GLOSSARY OF LAW SCHOOL TERMS 181

Mistake of fact:

Mistake of law:

Mistrial:

Motion:

Motion in limine:

Murder:

Nolo contendere:

Not guilty verdict:

Notice:

Objection:

Offer of proof:

Off-the-record remarks:

Opening statement:

Order:

Overrule:

Peremptory challenge:

Perjury:

Plea:

Plea bargaining:

Prejudicial error:

Preliminary hearing:

Preponderance of the evidence:

Present sense impression:

Presumption of innocence:

Pretrial motion:

Prior inconsistent statement:

Privileged, privileges:

Pro bono:

Pro per (also pro se):

Probable cause:

Probative value:

Prosecutors:

Public defenders:

Record:

Recusal:

Redact:

Redirect examination:

Regulations:

Relevance:

Relief:

Restitution:

Sanctions:

Seal:

Search warrant:

Self-defense:

Self-incrimination:

Sentence:

Specific intent:

Standing:

Statutes of limitations:

Stipulation:

Stop and frisk:

Subpoena:

Subpoena duces tecum:

Sustain:

Transcript:

Trial:

U.S. attorneys:

GLOSSARY OF LAW SCHOOL TERMS 183

Vacate:

Venue:

Verdict:

Voir dire:

Waive/Waiver:

Warrant:

Writ:

For students who are unfamiliar with legal terminology or who want basic information on court system and other foundational information that will be helpful for success in law school, here are some resources to consult:

1. https://Civics101Podcast.org

2. https://iCivics.org

3. Khan Academy at https://www.khanacademy.org

4. Legal English Resources page on Georgetown Legal English Blog—designed for non-English speakers but includes resources that can be very useful for all law students.

5. Nolo.com including Represent Yourself in Court and The Criminal Law Handbook

---

SAMPLE ANSWERS AND OUTLINES

SAMPLE OUTLINE of Question

Did Dan, Donna, Donald or Dalia violate poultry preparation rules? There are a number of applicable rules here relating to cooking and cleaning respectively. Each is discussed below in conjunction with each of the four potential rule violators.

Cooking

Here the facts state that the power went off 30 minutes into cooking. If a thorough and proper cooking of this poultry would have required significantly more time than that, it is entirely possible that Donna did not cook the poultry sufficiently. The reason for undercooking these poultry items may have been a power outage but the question asks if any of the chefs violated the rules, not why.

Beyond Donna, none of the others dealt with cooking so none violated cooking rules, but, as discussed below, some or all of them may have violated cleaning rules.

Cleaning

Cleaning rules include the requirement to clean both utensils and surfaces that come into contact with poultry, and the cleaning must be done with both hot water and soap.

Here the facts state that Donna did not wash the board or knife that came into contact with poultry. If Donna used these while poultry was raw, Donna likely violated the rule.

Note: the facts do state that Dan was on duty to wash dishes on Friday. It is unclear whether Dan's shift began before Dalia used the board that Donna had left out. But, if Dan came in before Dalia and did not wash the board that Donna left unwashed the previous day, Dan too may have violated the rule.

Dalia may also have violated rule in using "the nearest" cutting board and knife without verifying that they were cleaned with soap and water. However, the facts do state that Dan was responsible for "washing dishes and cleaning surfaces." If a cutting board is included in the "dishes" and something Dan routinely washes with soap and water, it is possible that Dalia should have been able to reasonably rely on Dan to have washed the cutting board before the "lunch rush."

In conclusion, under the given facts, Donna likely violated the cooking-related health rules, and it is possible that Dan and/or Dalia violated the cleaning rules, though additional facts may be necessary to clarify with respect to Dan and Dalia.

Finally, with respect to Donald, there are no facts other than that Donald was working on vegetable prep and sandwich assembly the day Patty likely ate the contaminated foods. Without additional facts, there is no way to conclude that Donald violated any rules.

GLOSSARY OF LAW SCHOOL TERMS 185

SAMPLE NOTES re: Question B

Below is an analysis of who will likely win the pie contest and why.

<u>Sally</u>

Sally will likely not win the contest because she ate with a spoon which necessarily required the use of her hands and thus likely violated the first rule: "no hands." Had Sally eaten without hands, she would likely have won. If the judges were to interpret eating with a spoon as not using her hands, Sally would win. She finished at the same time as Hal but she stood as required. She felt sick but did not show visible signs of sickness. And, she was 20 so did not need any parental signatures. However, given the plain meaning of "No hands can be used" it is likely Sally will not win.

<u>Hal</u>

Hal will also not win the contest for many reasons. First, Hal ate with a fork, which necessarily requires the use of hands. Next, the facts do not indicate that Hal stood when Hal finished eating. Hal also vomited immediately after eating the pie likely disqualifying Hal under the rule that "any visible signs of sickness will cause disqualification." Lastly, the facts do not indicate that Hal (age 17) had a parent or guardian present or had a parent or guardian sign his paperwork, both of which were required. For these several reasons, Hal will not win.

<u>Steven</u>

Steven is the likely winner here. The facts state that Steven ate "with his hands behind his back" and "dove face first into" his pie. Steven thus complied with the no hands rule (the first rule). Next, Steven stood after finishing the entire pie; the facts note that he was "standing" after having "licked every bite of filling and crust." Thus, Steven complied with the second rule which required one stand after consuming the whole pie. Next, Steven was not only not visibly sick but he seemed physically comfortable because the facts note that he was "smiling with satisfaction." And, last, that facts state that Steven signed his paperwork which was sufficient for the final requirement as Steven was 27, thus well over 18 and did not need a parent's signature or a parent's presence. Steven thus complied with all contest rules.

Conclusion

For the reasons stated above, Steven will likely be the contest winner.

SAMPLE OUTLINE for Question C

Note: It is strongly recommended that students outline an exam answer before writing so that the response is well-organized. The example below provides a detailed outline. An outline can serve as a first draft of a final answer, if typed, or it can be handwritten. Some students prefer to outline by hand on scratch paper and then type their actual answers. Experiment when you take practice exams and determine what outlining system works best for you.

Jimmy and Timmy Contest Compliance -outline of issues

JIMMY

- **feature someone seated at a desk**—Jimmy is seated "atop" his desk not "at a desk"—likely this will satisfy element.
- **be the original work of the contestant**—Does inspiration from another song make it unoriginal?
- **be created specifically for this contest**—Jimmy wrote this for his girlfriend, not for the contest. This might still be OK because the rationale for the requirement is likely to prohibit someone from using an entry for multiple contests. Does writing for his girlfriend violate the policy behind this rule?
- **be a maximum of five minutes in length**—Facts say it's "5-minute video."
- **be uploaded to the contest site.** Facts just say "uploaded"—Jimmy complied so long as he properly uploaded.

TIMMY

- **feature someone seated at a desk**—(there must be a desk—any desk—in the video)—No mention of a desk in these facts and Timmy filmed outdoors so not likely to have a desk.

- **be the original work of the contestant**—(covers will not be accepted); Timmy thought this was original, but it was not as it was "almost identical" to a previously recorded song.
- **be created specifically for this contest**—Facts state that Timmy "created the video for the for the contest" so this element is satisfied.
- **be a maximum of five minutes in length**—Facts say it's 5 minutes but that it has a the "5 second fade in and fade out," thus it may exceed the time limit.
- **And, be uploaded to the contest site**—Facts say "uploaded as directed" so OK.

Conclusion: Neither Timmy nor Jimmy likely complied as they violated one or more rule.

SAMPLE ANSWER for Question D

In order to be in compliance with airplane landing rules, Abby (A), Bob (B), and Cal (C) all must have 1) fastened their seatbelts, 2) placed their seats in the upright position, 3) stowed their tray tables, and 4) put away all large electronics." The analysis of whether A, B, and C have complied with all four rules follows below.

<u>Abby</u>

1) The facts do not state anything about whether A fastened her seatbelt. (Assuming flight attendant came by and checked on A while she was sleeping, it is possible that the seatbelt was fastened all along.) If her seatbelt was not fastened, A did not comply.

2) The facts state that A never touched the seat position button. Typically planes taking off have all seats in the upright position. It is likely because she never touched the button that the seat remained in the upright position the entire flight including at landing.

3) A's tray table had been open during the flight. The facts do not state whether she closed it. If she left it open, she did not comply with this rule.

4) A only had small electronics with her (assuming a tablet is not considered "large electronics") so she complied with this rule.

In conclusion, A complied with the electronics rule. Assuming A's seatbelt was fastened and her tray table was closed, and given that seats are typically in the upright position at take-off, it is likely that she complied with the landing rules as a whole. Additional facts are needed, however, to be certain as to A's compliance.

Bob (B)

1) The facts do not state anything about whether B fastened his seatbelt. The same analysis as discussed above with respect to A's seatbelt applies here with respect to B.

2) There are no facts at all that indicate the position of B's seat.

3) There are no facts that indicate whether B's tray table had been open during the flight.

4) B had his computer on his lap. It does not absolve B of this requirement that he had it covered such that the flight attendant may not have seen it. B violated the electronics rule.

In conclusion, even if additional facts might show that B complied with respect to his seatbelt, seat position, or tray table, B will be found in non-compliance of landing rules because his computer was on his lap, violating the large electronics rule.

Cal

1) The facts do not state anything about whether C fastened his seatbelt. (As above, assuming flight attendant came by and checked on C while he was sleeping, it is possible that the seatbelt was fastened all along.)

2) There facts indicate that C pushed the button on his seat after the announcement. Assuming it had been in the reclining position and he pushed the button with sufficient strength to make it upright, C will be found to have complied

with this rule. However, the facts do not indicate for certain that the seat actually moved into the upright position when he pushed the button. (There are no facts to indicate that the seat was reclined at the time of the announcement. C could have had his seat upright all along and pushed the button to recline it then. But, the facts do indicate that C heard the announcement so it can be inferred that his immediate action following the announcement would be to comply and push the button to move the seat to its upright position.)

3) There are no facts that indicate whether C's tray table had been open during the flight, but often people who watch movies on computers during flights set their computers on their tray table. If C had done this, the facts do not indicate whether or not he stopped and stowed the tray table.

4) C was using his computer during the flight. There are no facts to indicate that he put it away after the announcement.

More facts are needed to determine whether C complied with each of the four rules. With the facts that are known, it cannot be found conclusively that he either did or did not comply.

Conclusion

As discussed above, it appears that A likely complied, B did not comply, and additional facts are required to know if C complied.

EXCERPT FROM AUTHOR BERMAN'S *STEP-BY-STEP GUIDE TO CONTRACTS*

The *Step-by-Step Guide to Contracts* is an interactive outline and workbook designed to effectively prepare students to pass exams. The most heavily tested legal rules are presented in a format that mirrors the way they arise as issues in typical testing fact patterns. Rule statements are set out in easy-to-memorize statements, with a breakdown of the element components and logical steps to take to apply new facts to each legal element.

Fluency with the legal terminology is also essential to exam success, so this *Step-by-Step Guide* includes fill-in-the-blank spaces to help you learn and memorize definitions of key terms as they are introduced, and a glossary of selected terms at the end for further reference.

In addition to learning the law and memorizing key rules and terms, success in law school also requires the hard work of deep learning, engaging with problems to test your own knowledge, and working toward gaining a strong command of all testable topics. To that end, this *Guide* contains short-answer Test Yourself questions. Working through these questions and then reading the answers and explanations to determine where your understanding is clear and where you must do additional work will help you master the skill of applying the relevant rules to new and different fact patterns. In addition to the short-answer questions, this Guide also includes numerous full-length essay questions with sample answers—providing further practice to test your knowledge and deepen your learning.

CHAPTER ONE

Formation

The first and often most heavily tested area of contracts is: **Was a contract properly formed?**

Unless the facts say there was a valid contract, *always* discuss contract formation, usually at or toward the very beginning of the answer. Do not assume validity. A grader will never credit the spotting of an issue that is not explicitly discussed.

Remember that offer and acceptance is a game of ping-pong and that play shifts back and forth between the parties who are negotiating to form a contract.

> Always begin by assessing the applicable law: UCC and/or common law. See Introduction to Contracts Study Guide.

OVERVIEW APPROACH
Formation

In order for there to be a validly formed contract, the facts must establish that:

Step 1: the parties mutually agreed to certain basic terms;
Step 2: the agreement was supported by consideration; and
Step 3: there are no valid formation/enforcement defenses.

Formation—Overview Step 1: Did the parties mutually agree to certain basic terms?

This section involves the familiar components of **Offer and Acceptance** or "mutual assent" that exists after one party makes a valid offer (the offeror) that is accepted in a timely manner by the other party (the offeree).

> Fact patterns that test this area tend to include a number of communications between the parties. Always analyze each communication, in whatever form (oral, written, electronic) in chronological order to determine if mutual assent exists. Work through these communications applying the approach below.

MUTUAL ASSENT EXAM APPROACH

Mutual assent, the first main element in contract formation, can be most effectively analyzed in three main steps, each of which has numerous analytical sub-steps.

These main steps are:

Step 1: Was an offer made?
Step 2: Is the offer still open?
Step 3: Was the offer accepted?

Mutual Assent—Step 1: Was an offer made?

An offer is a promise to undertake a specific action which bargains for a return promise, a specific return action, or a purposeful inaction. If an offer is accepted, a contract may be formed (assuming all the other requirements are satisfied). The first requirement is that the offer itself must be valid.

A valid offer must be more than simply an expression of desire to later enter into an agreement. It must be more than an invitation to offer. An offer must create in the offeree the power of acceptance and must express a *present intent* to contract.

There are three steps in the offer analysis.

OFFER ANALYSIS

Step 1a: Did the offeror appear to have the requisite intent?
Step 1b: Are there any problems with the content (terms) of the offer?
Step 1c: Was the offer communicated?

Offer—Step 1a: Did the offeror appear to have the requisite intent?

In order to determine that the offeror had the requisite intent, the fact pattern must show that a reasonable person would believe a valid offer was intended. The offer must appear to be extended seriously, in such a way as would invite a genuine acceptance. Offers that are made as jokes or in anger will generally not create the power of acceptance in the offeree, unless a reasonable person would believe a valid offer was intended.

Reasonable person interprets offer as inviting acceptance. In order to assess how a reasonable person would interpret whether a particular statement or conduct created the power of acceptance, consider the parties' relationship and standards in the particular industry. Look also at the parties' performance or words with respect to an existing contract or prior contracts. (Facts regarding past business dealings of the parties, past history of

INDEX

References are to Pages

ACADEMIC PERFORMANCE
Grades, this index
Improving Academic Performance, this index

ACTIVE LEARNING
Generally, 53–58
Balancing active and passive learning, 53–54
Before and after class activities, 54–55
Learn about learning, 56–57
Listening skills, 54
Metacognition, 56
Outlines, creating your own, 55–56
Test taking, 57–58

AFTER ONE-L
Thinking Ahead, this index

ANXIETY
Generally, 79–90
Adequate preparation, importance of, 81
Burnout, 85–88
Calming habits, 81
Mistakes, learning from, 88–89
PIF reflections
    Challenges, 87–88
    Dealing with anxiety, 82
    Feeling your power, 89–90
    Mistakes, 88–89
    Study space, 85
Reframing, 82–84
Self-talking, 82, 86
Strategies for dealing with, 79–82
Stressful study spaces, 84–85
Turning panic into power, 81

BEFORE LAW SCHOOL
Generally, 1–7
Life logistics, 1
Orientation, this index
PIF reflections, 4–5
Pre-law programs and books, 1

BURNOUT
Dealing with, 85–88

CALENDARING
Daily habits, 118

CARETAKER RESPONSIBILITIES
Generally, 49–52

COMMUNICATIONS
Communicate respectfully, 114–115
Focus and distractions, controlling communications, 48–49
Promptly returning calls and e-mails, 116

CONCLUDING REMARKS
Generally, 169–170

CONTRACTS
Guide to Contracts excerpt, 191–192

COURSE SELECTION
Second and third year options, 156–157

CRITICAL READING
Generally, 17–23
Active reader reflection, 18–19
Differences with pre-law school reading, 22–23
Good reading habits, tips for developing, 17–18
Reading or writing challenges, 20
Think while you read, 21–22
Writing notes in casebooks, 19

DAILY HABITS
Generally, 113–118
Habits, this index

DEADLINES
Meeting, 117–118

DEFINITIONS
Generally, 171–183

DISABILITIES
Testing accommodations, 21

DISTRACTIONS
Focus and Distractions, this index

E-MAIL
Messages not always received or read, 116
Read messages from your school, 115–116

INDEX

ESSAY QUESTIONS
Exams, this index

EXAMS
    Generally, 91–92, 119–141
Calming habits, 81
Closed book, 120, 129–130
College tests compared, 57
Confidence and strategy note, 138
Dealing with nerves, 79–81
Draft letter to family and friends, month before finals, 63–64
Essay questions
    Generally, 120–133
    Careful reading, 120–123
    Concluding in the alternative, 122
    Improvement action items, 131–132
    Issue spotting, 123
    Outlining answer, 121–122
    Personal opinions, avoiding, 128–129
    Proofreading, 129
    Sample answers and outlines, 183–189
    Self-assessment, 130–133
    Self-talk and practice tests, 133
    Thinking while reading, 122–123
    Three step analysis, 120–122
    Tips for answering, 125–129
    Trigger terms, identifying, 123–125
Mnemonics devices, 120
Multiple choice questions
    Generally, 133–137
    Approach to answering, 133–135
    Common mistakes, 135–136
    Reflections, 137
    Right and wrong answers, understanding, 137
    Self-assessment, 135
    Timed conditions, practicing under, 136
PIF reflection, self-care during exam days, 141
Practice exams
    Generally, 57–58, 91
    Essay questions, above
    Incorporating into study schedule, 151
    IRAC-style practice, 106–111
    Multiple choice questions, above
    PIF reflection, 57–58
    Sample answers and outlines, 183–189
    Self-talk and practice tests, 133

Prioritizing study time before finals, 47–48
Ramping up for finals
    Generally, 138–141
    Confidence and strategy note, 138
    Skipping review of certain areas, 138
    Study and self-care, 138, 141
    Things to remember in exam room, 140–141
Secrets to success, 119–120
Self-care, 138, 141
Skipping review of certain areas, 138

FOCUS AND DISTRACTIONS
    Generally, 39–52
Awareness of where time goes, 42
Caretaker responsibilities, 49–52
Controlling communications, 48–49
Daily time sheets, 43–45
E-distractions, 49
How to enjoy studying, 47
Keeping commitments but maintaining flexibility, 45–46
Managing media, 48–49
Money issues, 51–52
Parental responsibilities, 49–52
PIF reflections
    Caretaking and other responsibilities, 51
    Communications and media tools, 49
    Daily time sheets, 44
    Finals, looking toward, 47–48
    How to enjoy studying, 47
    Time allocations, 39–41
    Time and money, 51–52
Prioritizing study time before finals, 47–48
Procrastination as time thief, 42
Reordering time allocations, 41
Study breaks, 43
Studying in different ways, benefits of, 46–47
Transition time, 42
Weekly time allocations, 39–40
Worthwhile and destructive distractions, 42

GLOSSARY OF TERMS
Generally, 171–183

GRADES
Correlation with bar passage rates, 146
Curve, grading on, 144–145
Fear of losing job opportunities, 144
Feedback from professors, 144

INDEX

Improving Academic Performance, this index
Keeping in perspective, 64, 143
Low grades in first year, 11–12

HABITS
Calendaring, 118
Calming habits, 81
Communicate respectfully, 114–115
Complying with rules, 117–118
Daily habits, 113–118
Deadlines, meeting, 117–118
Ethics and professional responsibility, 113–114
Exercise, daily routine, 160
Good faith errors, 114
Good reading habits, 17–18
Messages not always received or read, 116
Organizational skills, 117
Punctuality, 117–118
Read messages from your school, 115–116
Return calls and e-mails promptly, 116
Social media posts, take care with, 116–117

HARD WORK
Generally, 29–33
Persistence and attention to detail, 29, 31
PIF reflection, 33
Privilege of studying, 32
Time, protecting rather than managing, 30–31, 41
What hard work means and does not mean, 32–33

IMPROVING ACADEMIC PERFORMANCE
Generally, 143–157
See also Grades, this index
Athletics or arts analogy, 153–154
Bottom quarter of class, getting help, 150
Changing habits, 150
Cooking analogy, 154
Event planning analogy, 155–156
Feedback from professors, 144
Fine tuning or minor adjustments, 150
Fitness analogy, 151–152
Help, seeking and accepting, 147, 151
Jumpstarting studying, 152–153
Knowing your strengths, 148
Mental health issues, 149–150
Persistence, need for, 145–146
Personal finance analogy, 153
Physical health, 149

PIF reflections
    Generally, 145–147, 152–153
    Jumpstarting studying, 152–153
    Planning ahead, 155–156
Practice exams, incorporating into study schedule, 151
Reflections on first semester, 144–145
Small changes, suggestions for, 147–148
Study time, increasing, 151–153
Substance abuse issues, 149–150
Tackling concerns, 146–147

INTERVIEWS
Informational interviews, 36
Strategies, post-1L, 165–166

INTRODUCTION
Generally, ix et seq.

IRAC
Generally, 91–111
Analysis, 93, 95–96
Conclusion, 94
Defined, 91
Essay questions and sample answers, 102–106
IRAC-style practice, 106–111
Issue spotting, 94–95
Issue to be resolved, 92–93
Proof as synonym for analysis, 96–97
Rules, 93
Sample fact patterns, 97–102

LAWYER ASSISTANCE PROGRAMS
Mental health or substance abuse issues, 149–150

MENTAL HEALTH
Getting help, 149–150

MENTORS
Generally, 10, 13–15
Career mentors, 166

MISTAKES
Good faith errors, 114
Learning from, 88–89
Multiple choice tests, 135–136

MONEY AND FINANCES
Addressing in success plan, 159
Time and money, 51–52

MULTIPLE CHOICE QUESTIONS
Exams, this index

NEGATIVITY
Positive and Negative People, this index

NERVES
Anxiety, this index

ORIENTATION
Generally, 1–7
Important information, 5
Internal dialogues, 2–4
PIF reflections, 7
What to expect, 2
Whom to talk to or reach out to, 5–7

OUTLINES
Creating your own, 55–56
Exam outlines, 121–122
Sample answers and outlines, 183–189

PARENTAL RESPONSIBILITIES
Generally, 49–52

POSITIVE AND NEGATIVE PEOPLE
Generally, 59–77
Beginning law school, draft letter to family and friends, 62–63
Building resistance against negativity, 60
Cultural differences, 69
Expectations of others, 66–67
Explaining why law school is different, 65–66
Family dialogues, 68–70
Finals, month before, draft letter to family and friends, 63–64
Grades, keeping in perspective, 64
Happy hour dilemma, 70–71
Identifying supporters and saboteurs, 60–62
Negative encounter with professor, 74
Peer pressure, 74
PIF/CCC reflections
    Saying no, 72
    Self-sabotage, 76–77
    Supporters and saboteurs, 60–61
Practice saying no, 67–69
Productive ways to say no, 72–73
Rude behavior, 74–75
Saboteurs and self-sabotage, 73–77
Study buddy, unhelpful, 71–72
Undermining behavior, 59–60
Unsupportive classmates, 73

POSITIVE FOOT, STARTING ON
Generally, 9–15
Fixed vs. growth mindsets, 9–10
Learning and making improvements, 9
Low grades in first year, 11–12
Mentors, 10, 13–15
Positive changes, making before finals, 10
Reflections, PIF and CCC, 12–13
Reframing mistakes as opportunities, 10
Well-being, physical and mental, 10
Worst case scenario, 11–12

PRACTICE EXAMS
Exams, this index

PROCRASTINATION
Time thief, 42

PROFESSIONAL IDENTITY FORMATION (PIF)
Explanation, xi–xiii
Reflections and exercises
    Active reading, 18–19, 22
    Active/passive learning, 54
    Anxiety, dealing with, 82
    Caretaking or responsibility for others, 51
    Challenges, 87–88
    Concluding remarks, 170
    Cross-cultural competency, 13
    Daily time sheets, 44
    Feeling your power, 89–90
    Finals, looking toward, 47–48
    Finding your why, xv, 27
    Hard work, 33
    Improving from first semester, 146–147
    Issue spotting, 94–95
    Jumpstarting studying, 152–153
    Messages and media, controlling, 49
    Mistakes, 88–89
    Multiple choice exams, 137
    Planning ahead, 155
    Practice tests, 57–58
    Prior to law school and orientation, 4–5, 7
    Priorities, 12
    Saying no, 72
    Second semester, 145
    Self-care during exam days, 141
    Self-sabotage, 76
    Study space, 85
    Studying, how to enjoy, 47
    Supporters and saboteurs, 60–61
    Time and money, 51–52
    Transferable skills, 167
    Trustworthy people, 113–114
    Visualizing yourself as lawyer, 36–37
    Weekly time allocations, 39–41

INDEX

PROFESSIONAL RESPONSIBILITY
Daily habits, 113–114

PUNCTUALITY
Daily habits, 117–118

REFLECTIONS AND EXERCISES
Professional Identity Formation (PIF), this index

SABOTEURS
Positive and Negative People, this index

SECOND SEMESTER
Improving Academic Performance, this index

SELF-TALKING
Anxiety, 82, 86
Practice tests, 133

SOCIAL MEDIA
Take care with posts, 116–117

STUDYING
Active Learning, this index
Benefits of studying in different ways, 46–47
Focus and Distractions, this index
Jumpstarting studying, 152–153
Practice exams, incorporating into study schedule, 151
Prioritizing study time before finals, 47–48
Privilege of studying, 32
Ramping up for finals, study and self-care, 138, 141
Stressful study spaces, 84–85
Study breaks, positive effects, 43, 72
Unhelpful study buddy, 71–72

SUBSTANCE ABUSE
Getting help, 149–150

SUCCESS PLAN
Generally, 159–164
Daily exercise routine, 160
Elements of plan, 160
Financial literacy resources, 159
Money and finances, addressing, 159
Template, 161–164
Time management, 159–160
Updating regularly, 160

TESTS AND TEST TAKING
Exams, this index

THINKING AHEAD
Generally, 165–168
Career mentor, finding, 166
Course selection, second and third year options, 156–157
Interviewing strategies, 165–166
PIF exercise, transferable skills, 167–168
Transferable skills, identifying, 166–168

TIME
Addressing in success plan, 159–160
Daily time sheets, 43–45
Money and time, 51–52
Protecting rather than managing, 30–31, 41
Transition time, 42
Weekly time allocations, 39–41

TRANSFERABLE SKILLS
Identifying, 166–168

UNDERMINING
Positive and Negative People, this index

VISUALIZATION
Generally, 35–37
Courtroom observation, 35–36
Informational interviews, 36
Reflections and exercise, CCC/PIF, 36–37

WHY LAW SCHOOL
Generally, 25–28
Default choice, 26
Learning how to learn, 28
PIF reflection, 27